Buddhism

The Basics: 3

Buddhism

Herbert Ellinger

SCM PRESS LTD
Trinity Press International

Translated by John Bowden from the German *Buddhismus,*
published 1988 in the *kurz und bündig* series by
hpt-Verlagsgesellschaft m.b.H & Co KG, Vienna.

© hpt-Verlagsgesellschaft m.b.H & Co KG, Vienna 1988

Translation © John Bowden 1995

First U.S. edition published 1996
by Trinity Press International, P.O. Box 851, Valley Forge, PA 19482-0851.

Library of Congress Cataloging-in-Publication Data Available.

ISBN 1-56338-158-3 (Trinity Press)

First British edition published 1995 by SCM Press Ltd, 9-17 St. Albans Place,
London N1 0NX

Typeset at The Spartan Press Ltd, Lymington, Hants

96 97 98 99 00 01 02   8 7 6 5 4 3 2 1

Contents

1 Buddhism and Our 'First World'   1
   The historical Buddha   3
   A conversation with the Dalai Lama   5

2 The Founder of a Religion: The Origin and
  Formation of Buddhism   7
   The legend of Prince Siddharta   9

3 The Preaching at Sarnath: Buddha's Statement of
  Principles   16
   Who is Buddha? What is Buddha?   18

4 Karma and Dharma, Maya and the Wheel of Life   24
   The mysteries of the wheel of life   26

5 The Concept of God from a Buddhist Perspective   31
   There is no God in Buddhism   33

6 The 'Three Vehicles' in Buddhism   36
   The 'little vehicle'   37
   The 'great vehicle'   41
   The 'thunderbolt vehicle'   44

Contents

7 The Way of Buddhism in the Himalayan Countries 48

    The life of the Tibetan monks 55

    The Dalai Lama is not a god-king 58

8 Mantras and Mandalas and the 'Book of the Dead' 66

    Mantras are simply thoughts expressed aloud 67

    Mandalas are aids to meditation and not real
      objects of worship 69

    The dead return in the cycle of the elements 70

    The 'Tibetan Book of the Dead' 71

9 Buddhism and the West in the Twentieth Century 76

    Glossary 81

    For further reading 86

Buddhism and Our 'First World'

We live in the 'First World', and the rhythms of our life, which we ourselves have created, are more or less well adapted. That should not prevent us from developing some interest in ourselves.

What is Buddhism? A religion, a philosophy, a set of rules of life which make human society possible or easier to realize? Is Buddhism an institution, a 'church'? Can Buddhism also be significant for men and women of our highly civilized and highly technological world?

First of all, Buddhism is one of the possible 'ways inward'. Here it should already be made clear that Buddhism is far removed from presenting any exclusive claim and that it has no intention of recruiting Buddhists.

For a long time meditation and contemplation seemed to have no place in our world, so dominated by matter-of-fact technology, applied science and progress at any price. But here a change seems to be in the making, the discovery of a kind of thinking which will perhaps help us to find a way out of the split into which one-sidedness has manoeuvred us. It has often been said – and still is – that our modern life simply leaves us no time to go a little way into ourselves, and that the lack of time makes contemplation impossible. This argument does not hold water.

The 'way inwards' is less a question of time than a question of the will, of our own energy. Moreover, in a world which often makes total demands on us, where will we find additional energy if we do not even know that we can find it if we go 'inwards'? So whence are we to derive the motivation for an additional expenditure of energy, the 'usefulness' of which we do not know? We have established our values and also consolidated them to a high degree. But in this way other sources of our life have been lost; we have obscured and often forgotten them.

However, we are slowly beginning to understand that this 'way inwards' can mean joy, real experience and an extension of our horizons.

Our interest here is in Buddhism and getting to know in this thought world one of the possible ways which can lead 'inwards'. To achieve this we must open ourselves to an alien world, and that will not always be easy. We will have to recognize that people can look at and understand their world and themselves in quite a different way from that to which we are accustomed. We will have to note that our view is one possible view, but not the only one. We shall also see that there is something that unites people all over the world: the fact of being human.

In considering the phenomenon of Buddhism we cannot avoid using terms which at first seem strange to us — sometimes even nonsensical. However, we should not allow them to perplex us, but rather attempt to understand human thought in terms of them. So here by way of anticipation is a taste of concepts which are alien to us but are fixed points in Buddhist thought.

By karma Buddhists understand a causal principle which is a property of any matter, and therefore also of all life: any action, any failure to act, any thought, any absence of thought, results in the next action, the next failure to act and so on. Buddhists call this causal network, this causal determination the effect of which itself becomes another cause, the conditioning of karma. It is the cause of being, the cause of lives. The plural is not used here randomly: rebirth, incarnation, is taken for granted by Buddhists.

Dharma is an impersonal, absolute, cosmic law without properties. As it belongs to the Absolute or is the Absolute, it escapes human thought, which of course is connected to the sphere of the relative. So dharma is – as the Buddhists put it – empty, it is sunyata, the void.

Now Buddhist thought sees the task of human beings as that of bringing their personal karma close to dharma, the Absolute. Once, after many lives, an identification between personal karma and dharma has taken place, karma has lost its object and the state of nirvana has been reached.

We in the West are accustomed to ask for facts. How many Buddhists are there in the world at the present time? Here our love of numbers and facts can play tricks on us. A recent newspaper article reported that there were 312,500,000 Buddhists. But who counted them, when and how? Who can tell today how many inhabitants of the People's Republic of China would call themselves Buddhists; who can provide serious information on this subject for Laos, Cambodia and Vietnam?

Moreover such numbers and figures end in absurdity. The individual Buddhist schools do not offer any claim to exclusive salvation. For example, in the Buddhist view one can be fully a Christian and a Buddhist at the same time. Thus mixed forms have developed quite naturally, as in Japan between Buddhism and Shintoism, in China between Taoist and Buddhist elements, and so on.

So it is quite pointless to try to count the number of Buddhists in the world. However, already at this point it should be noted that the teaching of Siddharta Gautama Buddha is more or less extinct in India, the land in which it arose, where numerically the adherents of Buddha are insignificant. Against that, though, we should remember that thousands of Tibetan refugees live scattered all over

India in refugee camps. Roughly speaking, nowadays there is a southern Buddhism in Sri Lanka, Burma, Thailand, Laos and Cambodia, a northern Buddhism in Nepal, Vietnam, China, Korea and Japan, and the special form of Lamaism in Tibet, Sikkim, Bhutan and Mongolia.

The historical Buddha

Now a few words about the founder of Buddhist teaching. The historical Buddha was born in 566 or 563 BCE as Prince Siddharta in Kapila-vastu, a city in present-day Nepal. His father, Prince Suddhodana, gave him education appropriate to his status and had him married at the early age of sixteen.

At the age of twenty-nine – soon after the birth of his son – Siddharta left his family and attached himself to various ascetic teachers who were travelling through the land. At the age of thirty-five he experienced Bhodi, the awakening, enlightenment. Initially he was convinced that his insights could not be passed on, but after some years he set the wheel of doctrine in motion with his preaching in Sarnath, near Varanasi. Buddha Siddharta Gautama then spent the rest of his life travelling through the country, and gathered a steadily growing host of adherents. However, already during his lifetime there were disputes within this order and even attempts on the Buddha's life. He died around the age of eighty, probably of dysentery.

This bare biography should meet our thirst for facts. We shall see that the legends which will be sketched out in due course have essentially more to say about the people of which they tell.

We may ask whether this Eastern philosophy also has anything to say to us in the West. On the occasion of an extended private audience in Dharamsala, his residence in exile in India, I was able to put this question to Tenzin Gyatso, the Fourteenth Dalai Lama.

A conversation with the Dalai Lama

Question: Is there a possibility for people who live their lives in Western civilization to attain enlightenment, as Buddha Shakyamuni taught? What does Your Holiness think about the Buddhist communities in Europe and America?

Dalai Lama: When we speak of philosophy or religion there are no limits. Buddhism was originally an Indian religion, but then it reached Tibet, China, Mongolia and so on. In these countries the teaching took on the characteristics of the people in question and adopted their traditions. So a similar process is also conceivable in the countries of the Western world. Although the peoples and nations of the world are so different, they are all made up of human beings. Death, old age, sickness and suffering are the basic problems of all human beings, and there are no differences here. People may have made different arrangements, gone in different directions. Buddhism can be one of these.

Question: But what about the lack of competent teachers in the Western world?

Dalai Lama: That is certainly a great problem, and cannot just be ignored.

Question: In your view, is it possible to learn Buddhism without a teacher – so to speak from books?

Dalai Lama: That is very difficult and possible only with Sutrayana; Tantrayana quite certainly needs knowledge-able, competent direction. (Sutrayana is a form of teaching which keeps strictly to the canonical scriptures of Budd-hism; we shall come to the term Tantrayana later.)

Question: Do you think that there could be something like an independent Buddhism in the Western world?

Dalai Lama: Each form of Buddhism has its own cultural aspect, and without doubt in the West the European or American form would have to be adopted. Otherwise there would inevitably be an insuperable clash.

The view of the Dalai Lama, given here in abbreviated form, is interesting and at the same time a typical example of the largely undogmatic attitude of Buddhism. That this is strong enough to integrate alien traditions and cultures without surrendering itself has repeatedly been proved by the course of history.

Buddhism is the religion of a founder. It goes back to the historical figure Siddharta Gautama Buddha, who lived in India in the sixth century before Christ. The doctrine of Buddha knows of dharma, the 'empty', absolute, cosmic law, which has no properties, but not of a personal God with properties. Buddhism is largely free of dogmas. It has a high capacity for assimilation to alien cultures, without sacrificing its principles to a cheap pragmatism.

2

The Founder of a Religion: The Origin and Development of Buddhism

Long before the silk route had its heyday, caravans promoted not only goods but also thoughts and ideas through lofty passes and hostile deserts.

The sixth century before our era must have been a revolutionary age in highly cultivated and civilized India. The longing of people on the densely populated sub-continent for change, for social renewal, must have reached a climax then, when the history of India was already old. If we compared this period in India with what was happening in the history of the West, we might think of classical Greece, which with its ideas of society and politics has had an influence right down our history – down to the present day. Or we might think of the Achaemenid empire of the kings of Persia and their dreams of world power, along with their lasting influence on Central Asia.

Already at that time there were links between the nations. For thousands of miles, over passes covered with snow and ice, caravans transported not only merchandise of all kinds but also human ideas. The Himalayas, Karakorum, the Pamir, the Hindu Kush and Tienshan were never real barriers at that time for people and their ideas. That also applies to the sixth century before our era, a time when the silk route was far from having acquired its later significance.

But now let us go back to the India of this time. The Vedas

– once rules of life, continually developed up to the Upanishads – had long become rigid, cemented by the caste of the Brahmans. The Brahmans, and only they, could and might perform sacrificial rites for the gods; for a long time they had become not only the spiritual but also the real secular authorities. They determined the rules of human society, but had isolated themselves completely and rigorously from the population and lost all contact with the reality of human life. All social structures had become fossilized, the caste system was producing quite incredible fruits, and people had lost all room for manoeuvre.

Against this spiritual and social background two systems of thought now developed which must have been felt to be revolutionary in their time: Buddhism and Jainism. The fact that they were contemporaneous is certainly no coincidence, but more an expression of the human situation. The Jainist prophet Mahavira preached guidelines for life which have much in common with those of the later Buddha. Without going into detail here it should be said that Jainism interprets with exceptional strictness the prohibition against killing which also exists in Buddhism. Believing Jainas – numerically they do not play much of a role in India today, but are known as bold, hard and often rich business men – sweep the streets before their feet in order not to tread unintentionally on an insect, and wear masks over their mouths so as not to breath in anything by mistake.

But let us return to the man who was to become the Enlightened One of this age. Here we can only tell legends which, while built on historical facts, in addition indicate something of the thought of the people who tell them.

The story is ages old. It begins an infinite time before the birth of Prince Siddharta of the princely house of the Shakyas in Kapila-vastu in present day Nepal. From the stream of time a man reaches the shores of our consciousness, in our dimension of time, in our age which has forgotten its essential characteristic: time is not linear, but is part of a circle. History does not repeat itself, but time does; it does not have a beginning or an end. The little prince who was probably born in the year 563 before our reckoning had accepted infinitely many karmas and led many – infinitely many – lives.

The legend of Prince Siddharta

So it is also true of Prince Siddharta, who trod the earth inhabited by human beings, that strictly speaking there is no beginning, and consequently everything must have already been. But let us listen to the pious legend.

The procreation and birth of the future 'Enlightened One' unmistakably herald the coming events. In flowery language we are told that the one destined to be the Buddha was not conceived in a natural way, for already in age-old writings it is said that such bodhisattvas did not arise from the sexual intercourse of man and woman but from the power of their own karmic merits.

A brief text from the scripture Lalita Vistara should give a reasonable idea of the style of pious Sanskrit language, as far as it is possible to do this in a translation.

'Driven by curiosity, laden with the fairest vessels of incense, flowers and garlands, ointments, white lilies, scents and garments, the asparis, the supernatural virgins with divine bodies that refresh the heart, full of blessing which the fullness of good deeds and work conveys, left the abode of the supernatural beings and went to the city of Kapila-vastu, the fairest of the great places with its hundred thousand gardens. There in the flowery fields of Prince Suddhodana, rich in swans, in the great palace which is like that of the Lord of the heavens, the women with their white, billowing garments, adorned with the

spotless splendour of their merits, pointed with their
fingers to Princess Mahadevi sleeping in her room and
spoke to one another . . .'

That is how the description of the choice of the mother of
the future Enlightened One begins. Now as the princess is
chosen to be the mother of an 'Enlightened One', she needs
the consent of her husband, Prince Suddhodana: 'From now
on, my lord, I will observe the eleven moral rules, and
therefore, O king, you should no longer approach me in
sensual pleasure . . .'

The prince agrees: 'I will act in accord with your wishes.
Be without care, for you are beginning a noble life. I and my
kingdom will be obedient to you.'

Thus on a night with a full moon in the rainy season, a
white elephant comes to the couch of the Mahadevi where
she is resting.

Nor does the birth of the one who was to be the
Enlightened One take place naturally. When her time is
come, the princess walks in the gardens of the palace, in the
Lumbini Gardens. While she is entranced by the blossoming
branch of a tree, the bodhisattva, the future Buddha,
emerges from her side without harming her. He takes seven
steps towards each of the four points of the compass to
indicate symbolically that the teaching of dharma applies
equally to all people. The legend sketched out only briefly
here may give some insight into the thinking of the pious
men who related it. Time and again these events have been
taken up in an incredibly tender way by the artists of all
ages. This tenderness is all the more remarkable since Indian
paintings and sculptures usually have an openness and
directness which often shocks us. However, in the early
period of Buddhism there were no figurative representations
of Buddha. His presence was constantly indicated by a
symbol, the 'wheel of doctrine', his footprint or his foot-

stool. Only very much later – especially in the so-called Gandhara period – is he depicted in person, and then often very realistically.

If we look at the legends of the procreation and birth of the Enlightened One, we will immediately be struck by the fact that here too the course of nature is denied. This must surprise us all the more since Indians have always had a less prudish attitude to eroticism and sexuality.

But first let us return to Prince Siddharta, who now grew up at the royal court. Remarkably, Prince Suddhodana accepted him immediately as his own son and provided an appropriate education. Though he knew that Siddharta could not be his own child biologically, he seems to have taken no notice of this. He was disturbed, because a prophecy said that this boy would one day become either a great king and general or an important holy man. The prince preferred the first part of the prophecy, since he saw Siddharta as his great and powerful successor. From the beginning he surrounded him with every splendour and luxury conceivable at an Indian royal court, but also cut him off completely from the surrounding world. So the young prince grew up, was given the best possible education and was also carefully instructed in the martial arts of the time.

Another of Siddharta's father's tactics to bind his son to worldly things was to marry him at a very young age. But let us listen to the legend again. It tells us that when the young prince Siddharta married Yashodhara, he was only fulfilling a promise he had once given: in a remote age he had been a Brahakarin, a Brahman student. It happened that Dipankara, the Enlightened One of that world age, was teaching at the abode of the young student. Siddharta wanted nothing more than to be able to take part in this teaching institution, but where could he get the flowers that it was the custom to hand over, since no more were to be had? Defeated, he met a young girl who was holding five splendid hibiscus flowers in her hands. She gave him the flowers when he asked for them, but in jest added the condition that Siddharta must marry her in one of his coming lives.

Now when Prince Suddhodana had chosen this particular maiden, according to the legend the following thing happened. All the pretty girls from the first families of the land were introduced to the prince and each gave him a costly present that Suddhodana had prepared for each of them. Yashodhara was the last of the girls, and she had no jewel. Siddharta took a precious ring from his finger to help her in her perplexity. But the girl declined with a laugh: 'I do not need your jewel, Siddharta, since I myself will be your most precious jewel.' We might almost suppose that she had known about the five hibiscus blossoms.

So Siddharta lived his life in an 'ivory tower', without any contact with people outside the palace walls. His wife bore him a son – by then he was about twenty-eight years old – whom he called Rahula. Everything was evidently taking a pre-ordained course.

But the prince increasingly felt inner unrest, an unrest which he could not explain. Contrary to his father's wishes, he left the palace grounds with Channa, his charioteer, and Kanthaka, his stallion. Already mature, he now had the four encounters which were to change his life from then on so fundamentally.

He noticed an old man who was 'bowed like the gable of an old house', weak and supported by a stick, leaning against a wall. Here for the first time Siddharta had his attention drawn to the fact of transitoriness and old age. It is moving and at the same time strange to hear that the prince, who had grown up in his 'golden cage', had to be told about the phenomenon of old age.

Siddharta returned shaken to his palace, but his curiosity about life had been aroused. A little later he again left the security of his walls. This time he saw a man afflicted by leprosy and bent to the ground with pain. He learned that sickness and disease can affect anyone.

Of course Prince Suddhodana discovered his son's excursions and was deeply disturbed. He redoubled his efforts to bind Siddharta to worldly things. He arranged splendid feasts with tournaments and dances. But the prince's involvement in life had been irrevocably aroused. Once again he left the palace area in a golden chariot and had his next decisive experience: he saw people building a wooden pyre and decorating it with flowers before consigning a dead man to the flames. The sight of the corpse confronted the prince with the inescapable fact of death, of finitude. It was explained to him that all that lives also has to die. Deeply shaken, Siddharta had himself brought back to the palace.

On his next excursion he encountered a man clad in rags and with the hairs of his head shaven. The prince stopped and asked the man, 'Why, sir, is your head different from that of other men?' The itinerant monk replied: 'Because I am a solitary, one who has left his house.'

Of course we should not make the mistake of understanding the four encounters too literally. They are symbolic stories, and are meant to communicate certain notions: they are meant to describe how someone becomes conscious more or less overnight of particular circumstances and phenomena of life which for a long time have simply passed him by.

The subsequent story is full of poetic drama. Literally overnight, Siddharta leaves his wife, his son, his family, his palace and the whole of his life hitherto. Again the colourful legend begins and tells us the dramatic events. Siddharta secretly awakens Channa and tells him to saddle Kanthaka and ride with him. Then they ride out into the night. The hoofs of the horses do not touch the ground; no one in the palace must be wakened. The prince takes farewell of his sleeping wife and son only with a fleeting glance; he does not dare to waken them from their sleep.

They ride swiftly until the first pale light appears in the east. They have reached a small pool by which white, blue and red lotus blossoms are beginning to open their cups. With his bejewelled sword Siddharta cuts off his long hair as an outward sign of his renunciation of power, casts his precious garments aside and gives them to his companion with orders to take them to the palace and to ask his father not to make any attempt to follow. Weeping, his friend bids farewell to his master. Siddharta begs some rags from a passing huntsman to cover his nakedness. Thus he wanders, deeply changed within, towards the rising sun.

Before we pursue the way of Prince Siddharta further, something should be said about an age-old Indian practice which still exists today. There are three phases in a man's life. As a child and a youth he has to learn, and is a 'student of life'. Once he has grown up, it is his duty to have a family and to feed them. But when he grows old and his family no longer needs him, one day he will quietly leave his house. He will wander through the world with a begging bowl, practise asceticism and prepare for the next life, the life to come. So he is a man 'who has left his house'.

(In this connection one might also think of the New Testament. There Jesus says to his future disciples: 'Leave your house and follow me.')

If we remember the Indian rule of life briefly sketched out above, it may seem incomprehensible that Siddharta should have left his wife and child. However, at this point he was still young and knew that his family at least had material security.

In the sixth century BCE, India was an age-old civilization. The Brahmans, originally the second caste after the warriors, had a predominant place which made any social development impossible. People were caught in a jungle of caste rules, and there was no longer any room to manoeuvre. Two religious founders, Siddharta Gautama Buddha and Mahavira, were born at this time, and we can see them as the social revolutionaries of their age. As in a great many religions, so too in the pious life of Siddharta, who was to become Buddha, biological procreation and birth are dispensed with. And this happens although – as we shall here – believers see Buddha as a human being and in no way as a god.

3

The Preaching at Sarnath:
Buddha's Statement of Principles

However different human beings and their traditions may be, one thing makes them all equal: the fact of life and its finitude.

So Prince Siddharta became an itinerant monk, 'a solitary who has left his home'. He sought two ascetics as teachers, but soon turned from these gurus, since he noticed that they could not help him further along the way to knowledge. He scourged himself, and neither ate nor drank. Soon five monks joined him who were amazed at his rigorous abstinence. Siddharta declined more and more, and suffered severe pains.

Here is the legend again. The former Prince Siddharta lay dying in the dust of the street. There – apparently awakening for a fleeting moment from ecstasy – he found a woman bending over him weeping. Wet from her tears, he asked her gently, 'Who are you to weep over me?' She replied, 'For ten months, my son, I bore you in my body like a precious stone; it is your mother weeping over you.' Siddharta comforted his mother – whether she was a dying vision or reality is really insignificant here – and from that moment on renounced asceticism. We who have a matter-of-fact, critical and objective understanding know that this woman can only have been a mirage: the scriptures tell us that Mahadevi, Siddharta's mother, died only a few days after his death. However, for some people drama and reality coalesce and form a different whole.

When Siddharta took nourishment again, his five companions left him. They called him an apostate, mocked him and scorned him as a weakling. We shall meet them again soon.

Let us now take up the legend again. A woman dying by the side of the street gave Siddharta some of her shroud which she had saved for so long. He made a girdle out of it, since the garments of the hunter had long since dropped off him. A young girl – does our imagination play tricks on us if we imagine that she was Yashodhara – hears that this man is now taking food again. She prepares a rice dish for him and brings it in a golden bowl. Siddharta eats the dish and asks, 'What am I to do with the golden bowl?' Amazed, the girl replies, 'Do what you think right with it, but I shall give no food without a container.' Siddharta does not give away the golden bowl, but throws it into the river. In this story, too, it is not the narrative but its symbolic meaning which is important.

Already at least six years have passed since Siddharta left his father's palace and thus abandoned his former life. Now he wandered through the fertile plains of the Ganges and led the life of a begging monk. Then one day he watched a Brahman gathering kusha grass. This plant plays a role in Brahmanic ritual, since sacrifices are offered on it. Siddharta asked for some of the grass and made a cushion with it on which to meditate, under an old peepul tree. This kind of tree is now called the bo (or bodhi) tree – tree of enlightenment.

Siddharta adopted the posture of meditation and sank into a deep trance. In the night Mara, the devil, the negative principle, came to tempt him. He promised him all the riches and power of this earth if he would renounce enlightenment. Siddharta resisted the seductions of the tempter and rejected him uncompromisingly. (The parallel to the temptation of Jesus is quite striking and obvious.)

After forty-nine days of the most intensive meditation Siddharta now attained final enlightenment, as a result of which the prince and itinerant ascetic became a Buddha, an Enlightened One – as a cocoon becomes a butterfly. Thus arose a being who beyond the wheel of rebirths, beyond all dualisms, any polarity, has identified his karma with dharma. This Buddha grasped the course of things in space and time; he became a unity with the universe, with the eternal cosmos.

I shall attempt to define the concept of Buddha using our Western ideas.

Who is Buddha? What is Buddha?

A Buddha is a human being and not a god. That is important. So he is a person who has attained absolute knowledge, absolute enlightenment. For him his karma has lost its object, since it is identical with dharma, the law of the Absolute. Now there are different Buddhas – and this does not make things easy to understand.

First of all, each world-age has 'its' Buddha, its Enlightened One, who preaches dharma to people in it. In the Buddhist view there is no beginning and therefore also no end in our sense; one world age follows another and the cycle of being keeps closing. We live in the Kali Yuga, the 'black age'. The enlightened one of this Kali Yuga is Buddha Shakyamuni, the historical Buddha of the family of the Shakyas. The Enlightened One of the past age was Buddha Dipankara, and the Enlightened One of the next age will be Buddha Maitreya.

Someone who has attained enlightenment departs from the wheel of life and is no longer subject to the law of rebirths, but enters into absoluteness, nirvana. However,

Buddha Shakyamuni resolved to remain in the life that he had overcome, faithful to his mission, in order to teach people dharma, as Dipankara once had and as Maitreya will in the next world age.

Alongside these teachers of humanity, some schools of Buddhism also recognize spiritual, abstract Buddhas who are to be seen as aids to meditation and centres of meditation. Typical examples of this trend are the Dhyani Buddhas, who are the goals of a 'meditative centring'. We shall meet them again when we look at certain schools of Buddhism.

I have already used the term bodhisattva several times. Without wanting to anticipate here, I should already make it clear that the bodhisattva is to be seen as someone who in the course of many lives has attained a kind of expectation of enlightenment, of Buddhahood. We shall be looking in more detail at the term bodhisattva in discussing the ideas of the Mahayana, the 'great vehicle' in Buddhism.

Let us dwell a little longer on the enlightenment of Siddharta under the bo tree, the 'tree of enlightenment'. Does this not remind us of the 'tree of knowledge' in Genesis, the fruits of which human beings were forbidden to eat? Sacred trees and sacred mountains have been recognized since the beginnings of humanity. In human consciousness they have the function of serving as axes for the world which link the super-terrestrial, the terrestrial, and the dark area of the subterranean. Where there are no natural mountains as axes of the world, people build artificial axes, like the pyramids of Egypt, the ziggurats of Babylon or the towers of our Western world. Mountains, towers and trees are symbols of the links between different levels and spheres which offer themselves to human beings.

But now let us wander with Prince Siddharta, who became an ascetic, then discovered that asceticism did not lead him to his goal and finally found enlightenment in deep meditation, and became a Buddha, again through the plains of the Ganges. There even now is a 'holy place' which the British called Benares; the Indians call it Varanasi. It is included in almost any tour of India. The tourists are conveyed in boats along the famous ghats and wonder more or less uncomprehendingly at the piety of the Hindus, who take their ritual baths at sunrise. They cannot understand that here the deepest piety and very secular things, like the colourful advertisements for the famous soft drink, lie so closely side by side and are evidently not felt to be a contradiction.

From time immemorial this Varanasi has been a holy place, a place where the powers of the cosmos are effective in particularly concentrated form. So that is where Buddha went; he gave his first sermon in the deer park in Sarnath near Varanasi, and there 'set in motion the wheel of truth'. We shall not be surprised that legend assures us that his first audience consisted of the very five ascetics who had left him furiously and in mockery when he ceased his asceticism.

Let us now listen to the 'Four Noble Truths' and the 'Eightfold Path' proclaimed by Siddharta Gautama Buddha of the princely house of the Shakyas (Buddha Shakyamuni) about two thousand five hundred years ago:

'The Noble Truth of suffering, O monks, is this: birth is suffering; aging is suffering; sickness is suffering; death is suffering; association with the unpleasant is suffering; dissociation from the pleasant is suffering; not to get what one wants is suffering – in brief, the five aggregates of attachment are suffering.

The Noble Truth of the origin of suffering, O monks, is this: it is this thirst which produces re-existence and re-becoming, bound up with passionate greed.

The Noble Truth of the cessation of suffering is this: it is the complete cessation of that very thirst; giving it up, renouncing it, emancipating oneself from it, detaching oneself from it.

The Noble Truth of the path leading to the cessation of suffering is this: it is simply the Noble Eightfold Path, namely right view; right intent; right speech; right action; right livelihood; right effort; right mindfulness; right concentration.'

That is what Buddha Shakyamuni taught in the deer park of Sarnath. At a superficial glance one might think that he was preaching a way of repudiation, of asceticism, of a passive attitude towards life. But that is not at all the case. Time and again in his teaching he emphasizes the 'middle way' which cannot be either turning away or the unconditional and exclusive worship of the earthly (samsara).

After his first teaching in the deer park of Sarnath, the Enlightened One travelled through India and rapidly gathered an ever larger community around him. It was also in keeping with an old tradition that prosperous people gave lodging to wise men and their followers. These communities then spent some weeks or even months in the gardens of their patrons, who also provided them with food. Time and again some would then join these itinerant orders and follow their master for longer or shorter periods of time. Buddha Shakyamuni also gathered such a rapidly growing circle around himself, and an order formed. First of all this community of the followers of Buddha was a loose one, and it was enough to say the 'refuge formula' to join them: 'I take my refuge in Buddha, the Enlightened One; I take my refuge in dharma, the eternal law; I take my refuge in the sangha, the order.'

Buddha Shakyamuni lived beyond the age of eighty. However, his life was by no means harmonious. Ambitious disciples wanted to take over the leadership of the sangha as it extended further and further; they engaged in intrigues against one another and there were even attempts to kill the Enlightened One. The temptation kept growing to doubt the integrity of Buddha, to undermine his authority and to destroy his calling.

To return once again to the legend. One day, an apparently pregnant woman rushed up to the Enlightened One and accused him of having made her pregnant. But under the gaze of the Buddha the pillow under her dress with which she had tried to simulate her pregnancy dropped down and she went away screaming.

It is easy to see how Buddha would have made bitter enemies especially also among the Brahmans; after all, he was the one who unconditionally rejected the caste system. It is clear what this must have meant at the time if we reflect that despite legal measures, the castes have not effectively been abolished even today.

Siddharta Gautama Buddha died, probably in 483 BCE. 'All conditioned things are transient. Try to accomplish your aim with diligence.' According to tradition, these were the last words of the Blessed One before he went home to nirvana.

So Buddha was a human being, a human being who had attained knowledge and thus could become a teacher of men. Whether we want to see his teaching as a religion in the Western sense or as a philosophy of life, an aid to life and wisdom, is left to the individual to decide, though Buddhism – the 'church' which developed from Buddha's teaching – is now counted as one of the world religions.

Prince Siddharta became an itinerant ascetic. He had the experience that asceticism does not lead to knowledge and left this way. In deep meditation he attained enlightenment, and became the Buddha, the teacher of humankind. First of all he doubted whether his knowledge could be communicated, but then with his preaching at Sarnath he began 'to set in motion the wheel of truth'. The Four Noble Truths and the Eightfold Path are the foundation of his ethical and moral demand to overcome suffering. Thus they are a guideline for human existence and human society. Buddha now travelled through the land teaching and gathered round himself a community which increasingly felt itself to be an order (sangha). There were disputes among the disciples of Buddha even during his lifetime, and there were even attacks on the life of the Enlightened One. He then died at the age of over eighty, probably of dysentery.

4

Karma and Dharma, Maya and the Wheel of Life

All phenomena of the earthly world are relative, and therefore illusion. A personal causal chain, absolute law.

In the previous chapters I have used terms which are strange to us Westerners, although we sometimes utilize them. Now that we are beginning to gain a little familiarity with this alien way of thinking, it is time to go into them rather more deeply.

In the framework of the 'Four Noble Truths' we heard that suffering is an integral part of any life. It is caused by the relativity of all earthly phenomena. Nothing is absolute, and nothing exists independently in itself, so according to the Buddhist view nothing can be real. All phenomena which present themselves to our senses are therefore maya; in other words they are illusions, they are not 'real'.

Logically this insight also relates to the self, the 'I'. Tenzin Gytso, the Fourteenth Dalai Lama, puts it like this. The 'I' is a composite, dependent on space and time. Molecules and atoms which form this relative I were once an ingredient of other composites and will again assume other forms. So nothing is absolute, nothing is 'real' in an absolute sense; everything is maya and nothing has duration. However, it would be quite wrong to assume that this Buddhist view is nihilistic. Buddhists are in no way alien to the world; they recognize the importance of illusory phenomena and are not closed to them.

Now as I have already remarked, earthly phenomena – including human beings – follow an uncompromising causal principle: any action, any failure to act, any thought, any lack of thought governs the next action, the next failure to act. These conditions are the foundation of any being and are called karma. The web of karma turns the wheel of life, the wheel of rebirth; it creates the relative, the non-absolute.

The notion of karma involves polarity, duality, contradictoriness. All the phenomena which our senses can perceive are possible only in the field of tension of opposition. But in that case the duality is necessarily only part of the relative, not of the Absolute.

Absoluteness, the absolute law in itself, is dharma. A cosmic law of the Absolute knows no polarity or dualism. Thus contrasts in the sphere of dharma are invalid: being and non-being, life and not-life, light and not-light no longer exist; beginning and end have lost their meaning. Dharma is impersonal, since personification implies properties and these in turn imply opposition.

Now Buddhists see the meaning of life or, better, life, as bringing one's personal karma close to absolute dharma. Once karma and dharma are identical, then karma becomes inessential, since there is no polarity. This identification of karma and dharma is enlightenment, is Buddhahood, is nirvana. The idea that countless lives are necessary for this – time is relative and therefore maya – does not disturb Buddhists, since for them the fact of rebirth is a matter of course. For them a single life ending in death is incomprehensible and impossible.

But what is reborn? Not the personal I, the self, but the web of karma; it is the causal connections which are reborn. Buddhism no more recognizes a personal soul as we conceive it than Hinduism does. It is given to only a very few people who are already very close to an identification of their karma with dharma to recall their former lives, which then lie before them like an open book.

A few more words on the term nirvana, which is often misused. This is in no way a place, like a heaven; what is meant, rather, is a state which escapes description, as it belongs to the sphere of the Absolute and is therefore without properties.

The mysteries of the wheel of life

Now let us take a look at the bhava chakra, the 'wheel of life'. The bhava chakra is comparable to the triptychs on Gothic altars. Both were created for people who could not read. The pictures are meant to convey a meaning to these people. So they were – or are – intended for people who can understand a language of pictorial symbols. We Westerners have since largely lost this capacity. In a pictorial representation the six realms into which a being can be born are described; here the state of one's karma is decisive. We frequently find these bhava chakra depictions at the entrances to lhakangs, i.e. prayer rooms in Buddhist monasteries.

A 'terrifying being' holds a wheel with six spokes in its claws. Constant attempts have been made to analyse this demonic figure – which evidently symbolizes transitoriness. Some regard it as Yama, the judge of the dead, but probably it only denotes stubborn clinging to the illusory things of earthly being, the greed of the creature for being. Another view sees this figure as Mara, the devil, which grabs all living things to itself.

Three animals appear at the centre of the wheel: the pig as the symbol of ignorance and stupidity, the hen as the symbol of the senses and greed, and the snake as the symbol of hatred, dispute and hostility. These three symbolic creatures are biting one another's tails; their properties condition one another; they are the motive forces which keep the 'wheel of life' in motion.

Let us now look at the six fields of the bhava chakra: right at the top is the realm of the gods. As we shall be devoting a separate chapter to the definition of God, it need only be indicated here that these 'gods' are not free from the web of karma and are therefore mortal. In the Buddhist view it cannot be the aim of human beings to be born into this sphere.

The next field clockwise is the sphere of the 'titans', the asuras. Between them and the 'gods' grows the 'tree of knowledge of all things'; its roots are in the sphere of the asuras, but its fruit, which never ripens, is with the 'gods'. The warlike 'titans' love pomp and also lechery; their king enjoys himself with his wives. A green Buddha points the way to morality. These asuras are of course also subject to karma and therefore mortal. Sometimes we also find the spheres of the 'gods' and the 'titans' combined in one field.

Usually, if we continue round clockwise, there follows the form of the preta, the 'hungry ghosts'. In their human life they were narrow-minded, greedy and excessively covetous. Food and drink is piled high before them, which they cannot consume despite their fierce hunger; their mouths are too narrow. In popular belief these preta hover around the places of the 'sky burials' and harm living beings. As comforter of these tortured preta, in this field we usually find Avalokiteshvara, the 'lord of unconditional compassion'. More will be said about this figure later.

The lower sector of the bhava chakra usually contains the field of the 'spirits of hell'. This is depicted in a fantastic way, and the representations recall the pictures of Hieronymus Bosch. The damned beings there suffer equally from fiery torments and icy cold, and endure every conceivable kind of torture. In the middle sits Yama with a mirror in his

hands. If we look at this field, we feel compelled to make a
comparison with the Christian notion of hell. However,
there is a very important difference: there is no place of
eternal damnation in Buddhist thought. The 'spirits of hell'
in the bhava chakra will return to another sphere of life. The
Buddhist can make no sense of linear eternity. Moreover –
and this is certainly not easy for us to grasp – all the spheres
of the bhava chakra are maya, illusion, and therefore do not
really exist in an absolute sense.

Now – again clockwise – follows the sphere of the
animals. Ignorance, blind greed for being and weakness of
will can lead to someone being reborn in this form. The
pictorial representation shows the subjection of animals by
human beings; they are loaded with heavy burdens, struck,
yoked to the plough and – when they are used as working
animals and beasts of burden – even castrated. For us
Westerners with our own logic it is difficult to understand
how a being from this sphere can ascend into a higher form
of existence. The principle of serving and sacrificing oneself
seems to be regarded here as a possibility of improving one's
karma.

The circle now closes with the human sphere. Rebirth in
this form of existence is the one really worth striving for,
since only human beings have the possibility of actively
bringing their karma close to dharma and one day identifying with it. This active capacity is closed to the other forms
of being. So in the middle of the human field is enthroned
Buddha Shakyamuni, who proclaims dharma.

The border of the six realms of the bhava chakra is
divided into twelve zones which illustrate the links of the
causal chain. Scenes from everyday life are used as symbols.
Thus for example ignorance is represented by a blind old
woman, the drives which cause karma by a working potter,
the six senses by a house with five windows and one door,
greed and sensuality by a man drinking wine and so on.

(Buddhists recognize five senses which are analogous to our notions, and also add the capacity to think.)

Between the centre of the wheel with the animal symbols and the six spheres there is often a circle which is half black and half white. Here there is a reference to the ascent and descent of human beings during the forty-nine days of bardo – the 'intermediate state' between death and rebirth. We shall have to go into bardo and the Bardo Thodol – as the Tibetan Book of the Dead is called – at a later stage.

I have discussed the bhava chakra in some detail here, because this representation gives us some insight into this thought world which is so strange to us. However, any account here will be inevitably sketchy. It must also be noted that this description of the bhava chakra does not apply to all schools of Buddhism. My example – there is a series of variants – is taken from Tibetan Buddhism.

Karma, a term taken over by Buddhism from Hinduism and expanded, is a causal chain which is a characteristic of all earthly phenomena – and thus of human beings. In the human sphere it can be understood as a manifestation of being with its own responsibility. Karma has a place in the sphere of the relative, that which is not absolute. By contrast, dharma – which also derives from the Hindu sphere – is an absolute, cosmic, impersonal law without properties which the Buddhist imagines as resting in itself. It is the meaning of human existence to bring one's personal karma close to dharma and in the end to achieve identification. This identification is Enlightenment, Buddhahood, nirvana. The six spheres into which a being can be born are depicted in the bhava chakra. This 'wheel of life' can be seen as a symbolic representative of the world in Buddhism.

5

The Concept of God from
a Buddhist Perspective

**The gods are mortal and subject to the laws of karma;
they are one of the six possible forms of existence.**

Some say that human beings began to create gods for
themselves out of anxiety. The fear of natural forces drove
them to worship something. However, anxiety as the
exclusive motive for all religion is not very probable. Was it
not the principle of enthusiasm and shock that taught
people how to pray? Were not those creatures who developed into human beings and learned to reflect on what
went on both inside and outside them to some degree
inspired and involved when images and concepts began to
form within them? In this way they learned ultimately to
know the deity.

During the brief time – in the temporal categories of
evolution – in which human beings have inhabited this
planet, various thought-worlds have developed which for
all their actual or apparent differences have human beings
as a common denominator. We should never forget this
common factor and must always remain aware of it.

The Hebrew Bible, the Christian Old Testament, with
unprecedented urgency and drama depicts for us the birth of
the notion of the one God. This beginning then gave rise to
the three monotheistic religions: Judaism, Christianity and
Islam. They make the rigorous claim that they express the

sole truth, which they guard more or less uncompromisingly, and seek to impose their exclusive claim. Anything else seems to them to be reprehensible, paganism.

However, we should keep religion and confession apart; the latter has often been a motive force of power politics and still is. Arrogance and superiority have stamped those who think differently as inferior, pagan, primitive. So it is not surprising that the monotheistic concept of God was presented as the only one possible or conceivable. The 'poor pagans' were primitive because they had 'many abominable gods'. Hardly anyone seriously attempted to find a way into a different, alien way of thinking and thus make a correct picture possible. It had to be inferior, since that manifestly soothed the consciences of the exploiters.

In connection with the 'primitive' gods of India, I would like to quote a remark by an Indian wise man, Swami Sundrananda, from a conversation which I had with him: 'There are millions of gods, but God is only one.' We recognize that this is a problem of definition.

All the monotheistic religions provide their God with properties. God is omnipotent, omniscient, all-merciful and wise. But God also speaks in anger: 'Vengeance is mine, says the Lord.' God is also active: God creates the world and human beings, causes the flood, reveals himself to the prophets. It is God's properties which first make possible the notion of a creator God; the fact of creation necessarily presupposes this property.

This has continually posed considerable intellectual difficulties to theology and the philosophy of religion. One impressive example of this in the Christian sphere is the teaching of Marcion which, had it become established, would have given Christianity a completely different direction. The notion of a demiurge – a master builder between God and matter – as creator of the world – was time and again the consequence of difficulties of thinking of a God with properties.

However, we cannot go too far into the philosophy of religion and need to return to our theme, the Buddhist view of God.

As I have already remarked, Buddhism knows no personal God, no God with properties. Dharma is the cosmic, universal, absolute law. But the Absolute necessarily excludes polarism. However, a lack of opposition in turn excludes properties; in other words, the question of being or non-being is intrinsically superfluous. As the Buddhist puts it, the Absolute, dharma, is 'empty'. Buddhists call this void sunyata and conclude that all things, all phenomena including the self, ultimately rest in the Absolute and are therefore 'empty'.

I should point out once again that these ideas have nothing to do with nihilism. On the contrary, Buddhists are concerned with the world and are very well aware of the significance of earthly circumstances; after all, these are the substratum of their karma which they can shape, which makes possible their most intimate personal responsibility and imposes it on them.

There is no God in Buddhism

From what has been said so far it is evident that Buddhism cannot know a deity as we define it. So if we keep to our customary definition of God, Buddhism is an atheistic religion. Now in fact a quite unbridgeable contradiction necessarily arises: especially in Mahayana and Varjrayana Buddhism there are thousands of gods; an enormous pantheon of deities – including some with terrifying features – appears in the temples, speaking a strange and often obscure symbolic language with all their attributes and attitudes of hands and body, the asanas and mudras.

Now the contradiction is only apparent. The gods in Buddhism of whatever school are subject to karma and are therefore mortal and transitory. When their karmic merits are one day used up, they become mortal and will be reborn in another sphere of bhava charka.

These brief comments will already indicate that there are different conceptual definitions here. The same is also true of Hinduism.

Now let us return briefly once more to the bhava chakra. Yes, gods live a luxurious, carefree and fine life. But – and this is the decisive factor – they use up their karmic merits and then return to the cycle of life. We must note that different civilizations have different definitions of God. Thus, for example, to Muslims the notion that God has a son is an abomination.

Just a few comments on the pictures and statues of gods in the Buddhist world. Essentially they are no more than aids to meditation, and represent particular aspects of doctrine. These beings – whether they are Buddhas, boddhisattvas, gods, dakinis or yidams – are not worshipped in the strict sense. We can see them as catalysts for meditation. Those who are advanced in spirituality no longer need them; they can dispense with such spiritual crutches. In the Bardo Thodol, the 'Book of the Dead', the Lama also tells the dying man that the gods that appear to him are not real, but that they arise in him.

However, in this context it must also be noted that many pre-Buddhist notions have persisted in simple popular belief. Here beyond question there are transitions to what we understand by adoration. In addition there is belief in spirits and demons, in the effectiveness of particular oaths and amulets and much more – also of pre-Buddhist origin – that we must class as magic. Here the boundaries between religion, age-old popular custom and superstition become blurred.

Our definition of God cannot be applied to the Buddhist gods, which are thought to be mortal. So in the further course of our discussion I shall refer to 'beings', to avoid conceptual confusion as far as possible. Dharma is absolute, and therefore without properties and 'empty'.

6

The 'Three Vehicles' in Buddhism

Monasteries and orders come into being, doctrines form. All have the 'Four Noble Truths' and the 'Eightfold Path' in common.

There seems to be a certain regularity in the way in which human thoughts and inspirations turn into institutions, and religions turn into confessions and 'churches'. This has also happened to the teaching of the Enlightened One: a whole series of trends, of 'schools', have come into being. Here at least the most essential of them need to be explained – they are called 'vehicles'.

We heard of the sangha, the rising monastic community, in connection with the 'formula of refuge'. The very first monks collected and wrote down Buddha's sayings after his death. This gave rise to the first 'canonical scriptures'. I also indicated that even during the lifetime of the Enlightened one, differences of opinion and criticisms arose. Different viewpoints clashed very vigorously at the very first Buddhist council in Rajagriha, shortly after Buddha's death.

Today people keep talking about 'original Buddhism', whatever that may be. There were and are Western authors who praise Hinayana, the 'little vehicle', as the 'pure', the 'original', the 'unfalsified' form of teaching. Quite apart from the fact that to dispute the value of a school is utterly un-Buddhist, we should not forget that many thoughts of Buddha's have drawn in cultural and spiritual material from other, non-Indian peoples over the course of the centuries.

Two dimensions had an effect on the development of Buddhism, time and the geographical conditioning of cultures.

First of all the teaching of Buddha had to be distinguished from Hindu thought. All the principles had to be formulated and laid down in the first canon, the Sutras. But an elitist attitude of the monks which was there from the start and which later intensified led at a very early stage to the development of a kind of popular religion which developed apart from the pedantic speculations of the monks in which the people were no longer involved. Here already we can recognize the roots of the later 'schools' of Mahayana and Vajrayana. This development was furthered by the fact that Buddhist thought is largely free of dogma.

The 'little vehicle'

The origin of Hinayana as a more or less fixed unity is closely connected with the process of the settlement of the sangha, the monastic community. As I have already remarked, originally this group travelled through the land and stayed in gardens put at its disposal by rich sympathizers. People went there from round about to listen to sermons and teachings, and some of them then remained in the sangha if they were convinced by its teaching and way of life. However, things became difficult in the rainy season. Still, at a very early stage there were rich patrons who constructed permanent buildings or put existing buildings at their disposal.

This gave rise to the viharas, the monasteries. However, the monks in them often turned into zealots who increasingly shut themselves off and retreated more and more into the ivory tower of their scholarship. This gave rise to a monastic elitism with rules that became increasingly strict. It was no longer the teaching of the Enlightened One that was important; the decisive thing was observance of the regulations of the order which had become rigid rules. Institutionalized monasticism was proud of its ascetic way of life and its rejection of the world. Thus a trend arose within Hinayana Buddhism which was not longer really Buddhist, since the Enlightened One had always taught the middle way.

First of all maitri (friendship) and Karuna (compassion) were the leading virtues in Buddhist teaching. In Hinayana – concerned with the suppression of any feeling – friendships became indifferent benevolence and compassion and sympathy without any real feeling. Finally the 'little vehicle' took on an almost egocentric aspect which can hardly be seen as in keeping with the teaching of Buddha. Hinayana legends are evidence of this trend, in that they attribute to their heroes actions which are very difficult to understand.

Thus for example a prince gives away not only all his possessions but also those of his father in fulfilment of a vow. Then – when he is asked to – he also gives away his wife and children into slavery. It is difficult to understand such action as an act of ethical and moral love of neighbour. The prince exclusively looks to his goal, and wants to earn merit for the life to come by fulfilling his vow.

The doctrine, or the interpretation of the doctrine, of Hinayana became increasingly remote from life, from people, and became impersonal.

The theory of rebirth is thought through again in Hinayana and distinguished from Hindu ideas. It is not the I, the self, which is reborn but the web of karma. By this we can understand the field of tension between cause and effect: all actions give rise to further actions, and thus again become causes which have new effects. Once this chain is interrupted by the death of an individual, there remains a field of tension which is taken further by rebirth.

One could also say that the relativity of the subject-object relationships which our senses communicate, this karma – here I am calling it a 'field of tension' – continues to exist. The contact of our senses with the environment, including the self – leads to a bond. This 'force' remains after the death of the individual; it is reborn and 'seeks a new body'.

The world of Buddhist ideas is characterized by a high degree of peacefulness and a lack of dogmatism. Nor is it concerned to enforce rigid notions by a mission. So there have been no real wars of religion in Buddhism, no heresy trials and no burnings of witches.

If we look at the development of Hinayana at this period from a historical standpoint, we can see how it is closely linked to the hey-day of the Mauryan dynasty in India. Here in particular emperor Ashoka, who ruled between 272 and 236 BCE, zealously furthered the teaching of Buddha in his enormous kingdom, which stretched from Kandahar in present-day Afghanistan to the mouth of the Ganges. Ashoka was to begin with a pompous and power-hungry potentate who expanded his kingdom in a bloody way. His last campaign ended with the annihilation of the Kalinga people in the present-day Indian union state of Orissa.

Then, however, the personality of the emperor changed fundamentally. The warlike ruler became an unconditional adherent of the peaceful teaching of Buddha. Many viharas which he had built all over his empire are attributed to him. It is said of Ashoka that he had the ashes of Buddha distributed over his land in precious containers, in order to bring to all his subjects the blessing of the Enlightened One.

Cylindrical shrines with steps leading up to them – stupas – were built for these relics, modelled on the tombs of Indian princes and kings. These stupas have become the archetype of Buddhist symbolic buildings, yet have taken on the characteristics of the country in which they were built.

It should be mentioned in passing that the emblem on the present-day Indian state flag, the 'lion pillar', comes from the time of Ashoka. The original of this pillar is in the museum in Sarnath.

But back to the Hinayana, the 'little vehicle' in Buddhism, with its supposed closeness to original Buddhism. The texts of the Sutras from the original period of Buddha, written in Pali or Sanskrit, have often been lost. But they have been preserved for posterity by their translations into Mongolian, Chinese and Tibetan. It should be obvious that here quite a number of errors cannot be excluded, as a result of both deliberate and accidental changes.

Today, above all Thailand, Burma and Sri Lanka are indebted to Theravada – and thus Hinayana – Buddhism. It is hard to say what is happening in the religious sphere in the other countries of the 'little vehicle', in Vietnam, Cambodia and Laos. If we can believe the very few serious reports, then people have recently increasingly resumed Buddhist rules of life in these blood-stained and ravaged countries. As so often in their history, people have learned to adapt; for them it was and is a matter of survival.

It should be mentioned incidentally that the 'little vehicle' is also practised in Tibet, but probably only by learned monks. In Tibet the majority of people belong to the school of the 'thunderbolt' vehicle, often also called 'Lamaism'. However, Buddhists see no contradiction in the simultaneous practice of different schools. At any rate, in a conversation with me the fourteenth Dalai Lama emphasized that both forms were alive in Tibet.

Thus Hinayana developed at an early stage into a monastic science which was simply no longer understood by the great mass of believers. Moreover the monks largely shut themselves off from the outside world in their monasteries and no longer sought contact with the laity. The bhikkus – the monks – were so convinced of their intellectual and spiritual superiority that the laity were regarded as second-class, and even despised. They were really making precisely the same mistake as the Brahmans during the lifetime of Buddha.

So it is not surprising that very soon a popular belief developed which had its basis in original, mystical experience. This attitude presumably corresponded most closely to the tradition which combined the rationality and mysticism of the teaching of the Enlightened One. So we can assume that the material that is to be attributed to Mahayana, the 'great vehicle', existed right from the beginning and was not part of the learned speculations of the monks.

The first steps which are clearly to be attributed to Mahayana also claim to be sutras, i.e. to stem from Buddha Shakyamuni. According to tradition, many of the texts were at first hidden, since people could not yet understand them.

The dispute over the priority of the Buddhist schools – mainly engaged in by Western so-called Buddhologists – are not at all characteristic of Buddhism, since objective truth is itself intrinsically an idle illusion.

The 'great vehicle'

What are the essential features of Mahayana, the 'great vehicle'? The decisive characteristic is the notion of bhakti. One could reasonably translate this word 'devotion'. The leading notion is now no longer the cool maitri, friendship without real concern for the other as a person, which seems so worth striving for in Hinayana, but real dedication to one's fellow human beings, to one's fellow creatures, to the world around.

Moreover the 'great vehicle' says that anyone can attain enlightenment and thus to some degree stands in opposition to Hinayana thought. The way to enlightenment is narrow and stony, and many lives must be lived before attaining it, but in the end karma and dharma become a unity, and Buddahood is attained. In this way Buddhist philosophy has shown a bright and comforting direction, has as it were 'democratized' itself.

The Mahayana notion of Boddhisatva is closely connected with the principle of bhakti. In this connection the Bodhisattva is to be understood as someone who has attained enlightenment, Buddhahood, but voluntarily remains in the 'wheel of life' in order to help others on their way of salvation. So he renounces the fruit of his previous life, the aim of which was union with the cosmic law, nirvana. The one who has left the entanglements of karma and thus suffering behind him devotes himself to other beings who have not yet got so far on their way. (From this perspective Siddharta Gautama Buddha, the historical Enlightened One of our age, is also a bodhisattva. He remained among the living after attaining Buddhahood in order to teach them dharma, the absolute, cosmic law.) However, it cannot be said often enough that even a bodhisattva is a human being, not God!

Of the many Bodhisattvas who are postulated in the various schools of Buddhism I want to draw attention to two particularly striking manifestations by way of example, as they are particularly important for the understanding of the Tibetan form of Buddhism which we have still to discuss.

Many travellers will have wondered at a representation which can often be found, particularly in the sphere of Mahayana and Vajrayana Buddhism. It is of a person with many heads and a great many arms and hands.

What does this very exotic figure mean, and what sense do believers make of it? It is Avalolkiteshara or – as he is called by the Tibetans – Chenresi. It is the bodhisattva of unconditional compassion for every creature, as it were a personification of bhakti. The Dhyani Buddha Amitabha, the 'Lord of immeasurable light', gave it eleven heads and a thousand hands in order to be able to help human beings and all creatures. Its compassion is unconditional and immeasurable. So is it surprising that Chenresi in particular is the guardian deity of Tibet, whose people live their lives in unimaginably harsh conditions? Moreover Tibetans see the Dalai Lama as the incarnation of this patron guardian Chenresi.

Another figure is easily misinterpreted by foreigners. This is a person with a book in one hand and a sword in the other. The weapon is not, however, a means of spreading the doctrine by force, as one might assume at first sight. It serves to 'disperse the cloud of ignorance'. If we remember that in the Buddhist view this very ignorance is the cause of all the web of karma – and thus remaining in the 'wheel of life' – then we can understand what is being said here. This bodhisattva is called Manjushri. He is also thought of in a 'terrifying form' and is then Yamataka, the 'conqueror of death'.

Another word on the so-called 'terrifying figures'. All beings have karma in themselves and are therefore necessarily subject to polarity. It follows from this that beings similarly display two opposed polarities. The 'terrifying' aspect is often seen as the 'guardian of doctrine'. The rituals related to the 'terrifying aspects' are held in special rooms, gonkhangs, which are usually reserved for monks who have already attained certain spiritual levels. These rooms are rarely open to strangers.

The description here of two bodhisattvas, though it is necessarily only superficial, may give a little insight into a world of ideas which at first must seem strange to us. (Perhaps as strange as a description of Christian saints and angels would seem to a Buddhist!).

So we should remember that Mahayana, the 'great

vehicle' is characterized in Buddhism by the notion of bhakti, absolute devotion to one's fellow creatures. From this follows the idea of the bodhisattva, the notion of a 'helper to salvation'. Every creature has within it the possibility of attaining enlightenmemt, entering into Mahapari-nirvana. So compared with Hinayana, Mahayana Buddhism – as I have already explained – has undergone a process of 'democratization'; it has become more open and therefore more human.

The 'thunderbolt vehicle'

According to the teaching of Mahayana and Vajrayata ('the thunderbolt vehicle') the Buddhas have three 'bodies':

The Dharmakaya, the 'body of the law', is absolute, impersonal and attributed in common to all Buddhas – seen as a spiritual unity. It is undifferentiated, without properties, without characteristics and beyond any manifestation in the earthly sphere. So it is sunyata, 'void', in terms of Buddhist philosophy.

The Sambhogakaya is that body of enlightenment which 'radiates', which has majesty and dignity. It is peculiar to each Buddha and has nothing material about it; it is a spiritual being, a notion in meditation.

The third body of the Buddha is Nirmanakaya, the body of manifestation, the body to show. The Buddha makes use of it when he appears in the earthly sphere and teaches people.

We might follow this train of thought. A Buddha, an enlightened being, dwells in nirvana and consequently rests in himself, is without properties, for properties are inconceivable in the absolute sphere. Thus the being of enlightenment in the Dharmakaya sphere both is and is not at the same time. So it cannot be the object of worship – a cult.

From this notion derived the idea of the Sambhogakaya, the 'shining', 'radiant' body, which can be the object of worship and thus of a cult. However, the Sambhogakaya of a Buddha is a pure spiritual being and has nothing to do with the Enlightened One who in fact once dwelt on earth in order to teach people dharma. So a third body, the Nirmanakaya, must exist, the body which shared the destiny and needs of human beings. So when Buddha Shakyamuni remained among human beings after his enlightenment, he afterwards made use of the body with properties, the Nirmanakya.

Now let us now leave the field of philosophy, the doctrinal structure of the learned lama, and look at the further course of Buddhism. The doctrine of Buddha, built on the Indian tradition, history and way of life, spread beyond the frontiers of India. It necessarily came up against other cultures, peoples who thought and lived differently. On the high plateaus of the Himalayas – and also in the west of Mongolia – it came upon nomadic peoples with ways of life which had very different forms, stamped with animistic shamanism. In other words, there people believed in spirits and attempted to get in contact with them. On the other hand, in highly civilized China the 'teaching of the Enlightened One' encountered philosophies which were essentially based on ancestor worship.

Now from the start it has been a characteristic of Buddhism that it has not exterminated religions and philosophies which it has encountered, but incorporated them into its own system. This capacity for assimilation has never been a weakness but always a strength. Thus in the Himalayas a form of Vajrayana Buddhism, in the West often called Lamaism, came into being. In China, Mahayana became Ch'an, from which the Zen schools developed in Japan. The degree to which the teaching could adapt to the particular cultural soil of a people can be shown by the example of the bodhisattva Avalokiteshvara, whom we have already come to know as the bodhisattva of unconditional compassion – and he is only one of many. If we pursue the career of this symbolic figure with its eleven heads and a thousand hands, we come across a change in gender. In China is it Guanyin, a female deity. Here it is striking that this bodhisattva is always depicted in a sexless way until it takes on female features in China and Japan.

The readiness of Buddhism to accept other cultures is by no means sheer pragmatism, nor should it be seen as abandoning basic principles. The Four Noble Truths, the Eightfold Path, the notion of karma and dharma, continue to remain a basis, as does the theory of origin in dependence. We must not compare Buddhism with the history of Christianity or Islam, in which confessions have been and still are engaged in the bloodiest of wars. How different this is in the Buddhist sphere can be illustrated by the monastery of Gyantse in Tibet. There up to the Chinese cultural revolution eighteen different schools collaborated in the 'teaching of the Enlightened One' and thus showed practical ecumenism.

So Vajrayana is a further spiritual development of Mahayana, coloured by the culture and tradition of people in the Himalayas and Mongolia. The incorporation of these elements which were alien to the culture of India, the land of its origin, gave rise to these variants in the teaching of Buddha which now flourish. The 'thunderbolt vehicle' has taken on many Tantric elements. When these are particularly dominant, one can also speak of Tantrayana.

Monks in the viharas in the early period produced a speculative teaching based on the elitism of the bhikkus, and the people were less and less involved as the monks shut themselves off and retreated into their spiritual 'ivory towers' . This teaching, the Hinayana, the 'little vehicle', became impersonal and egocentric. At a very early stage popular belief gave rise to Mahayana, the 'great vehicle'. The value of bhakti, dedication, and the bodhisattva, the 'helper to salvation', characterize this trend. By the adoption of the cultural characteristics of the people of the Himalayas and Mongolia, Mahayana became Vajrayana, the 'thunderbolt vehicle'.

7

The Way of Buddhism in the Himalayan Countries

People up on the 'roof of the world' have given the ideas of Buddha a special distinctive note which exists even today.

Up on the enormous plateaus between the Himalayas and the Transhimalayas, between Karakorum, the Kunlun mountains and Chengshan, people live in conditions which for us are unimaginable. Their dwellings – where the people are sedentary and do not live in black yak-hair tents – and their flocks are often at heights of more than 15,000 feet. The splendid clear sky illuminates the landscape in colours to which we are unaccustomed: the mountain-sides shimmer white, violet, red and green, and the expanses of the plateaus range from yellow to dark brown. Narrow, ice-covered peaks and wilderness alternate, and wide areas are covered with salt lakes. The ground is sparse, and the yaks, an important basis for human life, need enormous areas of pasture, since the plants are so sparse.

Here and there small oases, a few hundred square yards of cultivable land, can be found. There people have taken the stones away from the surface, and built little walls round the fields in order to keep off some of the wind which rapidly carries away the earth. There they plant barley, the basis for the staple diet of those who live on the high plateaus, tsampa. They roast grains of barley, grind them and mix the flour with some fatty yak-butter tea to form small lumps that they can put in their mouths. If the harvest has been in any way a good one, they may even ferment some of the barley. The result is a top-fermented beer, cloudy and not very attractive to us, which we may taste when enjoying the hospitality of these people. On such occasions this beer, called chag, will then go the rounds. Tsampa is the main form of food. The yak-butter tea is prepared in long cylindrical wooden vessels. First tea is made – but not poured out – in them, and then it is mixed with some precious salt and soda. Then a bit of yak butter is added which is emulsified by mashing the brew. The yak butter is prepared and gathered on the pastures all through the year. Then it is put in yak stomachs and brought down to the valley in them. If one cuts off a bit of yak butter, it has striking patterns of mould in it, like Gorgonzola, and gives off an extremely rancid smell. For us, Tibetan yak-butter tea takes a great deal of getting used to. However, the inhabitants of the plateau drink great masses of it, since it is one of their most important sources of calories.

For good reasons, the houses in the little hamlets are sunk deep in the ground, so that the winter storms affect them as little as possible. Below them are the stables, so that a little of the warmth or the living room and bedroom above reaches them. There is a fireplace, and its smell penetrates the building. However, fuel is a precious rarity, since there are no trees to burn here. Thistles are collected throughout the year and piled on the roof. They are fuel, but also serve to provide insulation for the roof. But far more important than the thistles is yak dung. This is carefully collected, mixed with barley straw, formed into cakes and stuck to the house walls. In the extremely dry air these cakes dry quickly and drop off the wall. They too are piled up to provide precious fuel.

At these heights nature is of an almost unimaginable harshness for is. A cold winter with very little snow roars over the land with ice- and sand-storms. Variations of temperature of forty degrees Celsius between day and night are also quite frequent in summer. The plateaus north of the main range of the Himalayas have very little rain. The monsoon clouds coming from the south very rarely surmount the gigantic mountains. Rare storms which are as a result all the more powerful make the caravan paths disappear, and when the snows melt, tiny trickles become impassable raging torrents, which once again change the land.

We can understand that in the circumstances outlined here notions developed of nature having spirits. People thought they could recognize the demons of earth, air and water, and it therefore had to be assumed that all these powers had to be assuaged and brought under control by sacrifice and worship. The shamans had the knowledge and capacities to do this. Only they were in a position to make contact with the spirits – both the benevolent and the harmful ones – , offer the right sacrifices and banish the demons by spells.

This world of ideas is not specifically Tibetan, but originally developed in all civilizations. The features common to peoples living geographically far apart – we might think of the original population of America and the Mongolians – are on the one hand surprising but on the other simple to explain. Human beings with their increasing capacity to reflect and reflect on themselves are the same everywhere: they see their environment and themselves and attempt to explain both.

There were different forms of life with an animistic shamanistic stamp in the Himalayas in the pre-Buddhist period, which are summed up under the name Bön. However, this Bön was only summarized in a simplified form and written down after Buddhism reached Tibet, by a man called Shenrab.

Today there are still isolated Bön monasteries in Tibet. However, the present-day teaching of the Bön monks is not very different from Buddhist teachings. Still, one external feature of ritual is striking. Whereas a Buddhist will always go round a sanctuary, a stupa or a mani wall clockwise, adherents of Bön always take the opposite direction.

The Buddhist sages who went north thus encountered the animistic, shamanistic world of the bons, who had not yet reformed. What may have happened here can be explained by two legends, which certainly have a historical basis.

The Indian itinerant monk Nyamagun found a deep lake in the middle of a barren wilderness. But in the water there were no fish, only lu snakes, demons hostile to human beings. Nyamagun lay down on the shore of this uncanny water and meditated there for several years. Then one day he scattered grains of barley on the surface of the water and lo and behold, a right-handed swastika formed – an age-old Indian symbol of light and a Buddhist sign. Now Nyamagan said the mantra of Avalokiteshvara, the Om Mani Padme Hum, as a formula of meditation, and the waters flowed away.

Even now, travellers will be shown some petrified waves of the lake near Lamayaru Gumpa, the Yundrin, the 'swastika monastery', in present-day Ladakh. Nyamagun is regarded as the founder of this monastery complex, which today dominates a fertile valley. In the old rooms of the monastery one can still see the demons, who as 'terrifying beings' became the guardians of the teaching of the Enlightened One.

Another legend tells how once upon a time near Sakya in southern Tibet there lived a demon called Pehar, who did great harm to people there. But one day they succeeded in catching Pehar in a 'spirit trap' and throwing it – and him –

into the river. This baneful package now came ashore near
the present-day monastery of Nechung, not far from
Lhasa. A curious young monk made the terrible mistake of
opening the 'spirit trap'. Pehar went into a nearby tree with
a loud shout. In their great distress the anxious people
summoned a great Buddhist lama, Padmasambhava, to help
them. His spiritual power managed to turn Pehar round and
make him a guardian of the teaching of Buddha. Since then
when summoned in a solemn ceremony he speaks through
the oracular monk of Nechung and announces the future.
As late as the 1950s questions were asked of this oracle
before all important Tibetan state affairs, and even now in
Nechung Gampa people are shown the remains of the tree
into which the demon once went.

There is a story that the oracle of Nechung prophesied
that the present Dalai Lama, the fourteenth, was the last of
the series of incarnations of the Avalokiteshvara. In a
conversation with me the Dalai Lama contradicted this
version. He himself, he said, had indicated the possibility of
ending the series of incarnations during negotiations with
the Chinese. By doing so he wanted to make it clear that the
debate was not over the institution of the Dalai Lama but
exclusively over the fate of the Tibetan people.

Both legends – chosen from many – tell us that pre-
Buddhist Bön ideas, Bön demons, have not been eradicated
but put to the service of Buddhism.

So we should note that as in other countries, so too in
Tibet Buddhism penetrated without obliterating indigenous
religions.

Soon monastic communities formed in Tibet. Their order
called and still calls them Nyingmapas, 'the school of the
old', the 'red hats'. After what has been said, it is not
surprising that in these schools going back to Padmasambhava there were magical practices which represented a
danger in so far as they threatened to undermine the

distinctive spirituality of Buddhism. That is also the reason why time and again wise monks strove for reforms which ultimately led to the four orders that still exist today. Alongside the Nyingmapas, the Kagyupa and the Shakya also belonged to the so-called 'red-hat order'.

The great reformer of Tibetan monasticism lived at the end of the fourteenth century. His name was Tsongkhapa, the 'monk from onion valley'. The Gelugpa order, which really first created Tibetan theocracy, derives from him. This 'yellow-hat order' became constitutional, and both the Dalai Lama and the Panchen Lama belong to it. The reasons for the Tsongkhapa reforms were clear: the 'red-hat' order had become markedly secularized, and magical practices were obscuring doctrine.

Tsongkhapa reformed monasticism very thoroughly. Whereas the monks of the other orders were married and lived with their families in the monasteries, the Gelugpas practise strict celibacy. The monks are subject to strict discipline and order, and magical practices are largely rejected. Very soon after the reform the three 'state monasteries' of Sera, Drepung and Ganden came into being.

Vajrayana Buddhism – the 'thunderbolt vehicle' practised in the Himalayan countries, is sometimes also called Tantrayana. This is meant to indicate that it contains Tantric elements, some of which are even leading notions. But what is Tantra, what are we to understand by this term which is often misunderstood and quite frequently condemned as 'sensationalism' with marked erotic connotations?

Tantrism is not 'self-fulfilment by a heightened experience of the 'sexual act', nor is it a 'sexual way to human liberation', But it can be no coincidence that I have now already used the word sex twice in connection with the Tantra. An etymological analysis of the word shows that the syllable tan means 'extend', 'increase' and the main word Tana means threat and also 'extension'. There are two main translations of the word Tantra: 'prescribed' or 'normed', and 'playing on strings'.

If we follow the most usual definition of Tantra, we shall describe this trend of thought as a way which sees the capacity of human experiences as a means for attaining redemption. There are different classes of Tantra, and a distinction is also made between 'father' and 'mother' Tantra, depending whether the emphasis is on the male or the female principle. It can hardly be disputed that Tantric practices are also misused or were – indeed still are – the pretext for sexual excesses.

Tantric symbolism plays an unmistakable role in the rituals of Tibetan Buddhism. Here too we must once again limit ourselves to some examples to illustrate what has been said. A ritual object has given its name to Vajrayana, the vajra.

This is a sceptre-like object, usually made of bronze but sometimes made of silver or gold, which bears on it the symbolism of the five points of the compass, the four familiar to us and a fifth which indicates the transcendent. These five directions meet at the point of the Absolute and fuse there. The vajra – often translated misleadingly as 'thunderbolt' – represents the male principle in the world of phenomena and is carried by the lama who directs the ceremony.

A further ritual object which has its roots in Tantric thought is the ghanta, a bell the handle of which again depicts the upper part of the vajra. The ghanta is a symbol of the feminine principle of manifestations. Its ringing can always be heard in a Tantric sacrifice when the 'terrifying' aspects of a deity are invoked.

Tantric elements are particularly clear in representations of yab-yum. Yab-yum means 'father-mother'. Male and female beings are shown in sexual union. This fusion of different dualistic, opposed principles symbolizes the abolition of polarity, the attainment of dharma knowledge.

Here I am quite deliberately using the term being and avoiding the words god or deity, which could be completely misunderstood. Nor should we forget that all these beings are ultimately maya; they do not really exist, but are spiritual beings, helps to meditation which arise within us. But it should be said that these beings have a status in popular belief comparable to our saints. They too are 'worshipped'. Those who are advanced spiritually no longer need all these beings.

The life of the Tibetan monks

The life of monks in the monasteries of Tibet and their rituals changed after the occupation of their country by the Chinese. Before the terrors of the Cultural Revolution, this was the picture.

Natural land for growing crops and pasturing flocks is rare on the Tibetan plateau. So it must be the aim of a social order to avoid as far as possible dividing up the areas that could be used. Two customs were of decisive importance in this respect and meant that there was no population explosion in the Himalayas.

The social order of the Tibetans recognized polyandry. One woman married several men, usually brothers. Children from such marriages were always regarded as descendants of the oldest husband and were treated as such hereditarily. Alongside this form of family there was also polygamy, but it was probably practised much more rarely than polyandry. Now the Chinese have banned both forms. It is hard to say whether this prohibition is really effective.

A further important factor in the Tibetan social order was the fact that a very considerably portion of the men – it is said roughly a quarter – were monks. By far the largest number of them entered the Gelugpa order, which had a strictly celibate rule.

How did someone become a monk? A boy from a Tibetan family was usually given to a monastery at the age of eight, and initially the parents had to pay for his board and lodging. Over the years the boy then became so to speak a servant of a lama (lama means teacher, equivalent to the Indian guru). So it is not surprising that the material resources of the parents were not without influence. Well-to-do parents could get a good teacher for their son who was then really concerned to train him and educate him. The lama gave the pupil monk – the Tibetans call him getsul – at least the basic ideas of reading and writing. This was done predominantly by means of the canonical texts of the Kangyur and the Tengyur. If the pupil then passed certain examinations, usually at the age of between eighteen and twenty he was consecrated a monk, a gelong. Most monks remained at this level of the hierarchy; they were given particular functions in the monastery in accordance with their capabilities. As the large monasteries were also businesses, there were many possibilities for the gifted monk. Thus these monasteries often carried on trade with remote partners, and caravans transporting salt and yak wool were often on the road for years before they returned to their monastery with goods from Kashmir or India.

However, particularly gifted monks had the possibility of further study in the 'theological faculties' of the great monasteries – provided they were encouraged to this by those in charge of them. Usually already around thirty, they then achieved the degree of a geshe, a 'doctor of philosophy'. The abbots of the monasteries were recruited from these elites and the high positions in the Tibetan state were frequently occupied by geshes.

To this brief description of the monastic hierarchy in Tibet must be added the comment that many monks preferred an ascetic life with a purely spiritual orientation. They often spent large parts of their lives in lonely areas, exclusively dedicated to meditation. Quite often the abbot of a monastery would retreat for a time – often years – into solitude. In connection with the monastic hierarchy a word also needs to be said about the phenomenon of the trulku. A trulku is someone who has already come very near to enlightenment in the course of many lives. The trulku often has the gift of being able consciously to survey his previous life; he can 'remember' himself. Many abbots of Tibetan monasteries are such trulkus, and their rebirth is looked for again in a new body after their deaths. This is also true of the Dalai Lama.

Now let us look once again at a puja, a sacrificial ritual, in one of the lhakangs, the prayer rooms of a Tibetan monastery. I shall attempt to convey the atmosphere that we outsiders would find there.

When the first strips of light over the mountains signal dawn, the morning puja, morning prayer, begins. The lamas, gelongs and getsuls in their rust-coloured garments gather in the lhakang, to which is attached a figure room, usually dominated by a large statue of Buddha. There is no altar as we would understand it here. On the walls, frescoes depict scenes from the life of Buddha where thangkas, scrolls with religious content, are not hung on them. These thangkas are aids to meditation and lead the person meditating to the centre in accordance with quite definite rules.

The monks adopt the 'lotus position' with legs crossed under them on the low benches which are arranged longways in the room. The lama presiding sits on a yellow, elevated seat to the left of the central axis of the lhakang. The whole room is dark, and just a little light comes in from an opening in the middle of the roof. The many butter lamps give only sparse light. These butter lamps and the many incense sticks give off an intense, intoxicating smell.

The monks still talk together, then suddenly everything becomes still. The rhythm of muffled drums and the scanned texts from the Kangyur gradually command the observer's attention, even if he cannot understand the language. This dominant impression is further intensified by the fact that the rhythmic emphasis and also the pitch of each individual syllable obey rules which are strictly observed. After some time this murmuring increases and cymbals and bells become almost painfully loud. But suddenly the prayers break off and silence falls. Disciples go through the ranks of the monks and pour butter tea from splendid copper cans into the small wooden bowls which each monk has. Before them is also a small leather container with roast barley meal, which is now mixed with the butter tea. This tsampa is now something like a ritual meal within the framework of the sacrifice.

The rhythmic prayers begin again a little later. This rhythm becomes more rapid, the noise increases, and alongside the drumming now shrill shawms and flutes accompany the monks as they pray. It all swells to a symphony which does not sound very attractive to our ears, and the ghantas join in. We know that now the 'terrifying deities', the guardians of the teaching of Buddha, are being called on. The long tubes like alpine horns, with their extremely deep tone, sound out dully.

Then it all suddenly breaks off, and the resultant silence is almost painful. But the monks leave the lhakang clapping, to go to their daily work.

The Dalai Lama is not a god-king

Time and again one hears and reads about the Dalai Lama as the 'god-king'. That is misleading, since the Tibetans do not see their head of state as a god in the sense of our definition of God. For them he is an incarnation – in this case we should translate this word 'earthly birth' – of the bodhisattva Avalokiteshvara. The Tibetans also lovingly call the Dalai Lama Kundun, which means 'presence'.

First of all let us look at the institution of the Dalai Lama historically. In the sixth century BCE a kingdom began to develop in Tibet whose kings did not live in the present capital, Lhasa, but in the Yarlung valley. This Tibetan kingdom was so powerful that it could even conquer the then Chinese capital Chang'an, present-day Xi'an – though only for a brief period.

The introduction of Buddhism into the Tibetan plateau falls in this period of the powerful Yarlung kings (seventh to ninth century) under king Songtsen Gampo. Then, however, came a time of bloody persecution of Buddha's doctrine under king Langdharma. There was even a political murder: a Buddhist monk stabbed this king who was hostile to Buddha.

Then under the ruler Tritsug Detsen the teaching began to spread in a new wave. When the Yarlung dynasty fell, the unity of Tibet was also lost, and the individual provinces more or less led lives of their own. In the process two centres began to crystallize: the province of Ü with its capital Lhasa, and the province of Tsang with its capital of Shigatse. During these years Buddhism spread increasingly, monasteries came into being and formed spiritual, intellectual, economic and also political centres. Tsongkhapa (1357–1419) was then the great reformer of monasticism and the founder of the Gelugpa school, the 'yellow hats'.

The title of Dalai Lama was first bestowed by the Mongolian ruler Altan Khan on the then abbot of the Gelugpa and posthumously on his two predecessors. The close links of the Dalai Lama to the Mongolian empire will have played a significant role in the development of the secular power of the Gelugpa order. In the seventeenth century the Potala was then built on the Marpo Ri, the Red Hill. This was the winter residence of the Dalai Lamas and an expression of their power in the spiritual and secular spheres. (Long before the erection of the Potala, an imposing complex of buildings had stood on this island-like mountain in Lhasa, since King Songtsen Gampo had already had a castle and a palace built there.)

So the Dalai Lamas are incarnations of the bodhisattva Avalokiteshvara. But they are also trulkus, i.e. rebirths of themselves. When a Dalai Lama dies, the Tibetans say, 'He is changing his body.' When an adviser pointed out to the Dalai Lama that his predecessors had made different decisions on a question, he replied: 'Who is my predecessor? Am not I my predecessor?'

Time and again there is puzzlement over how the new incarnation, the new body of a Dalai Lama, can be found. So I shall tell the story of Tenzin Gyatso, the fourteenth Dalai Lama, who now lives in exile in India.

When the Thirteenth Dalai Lama (1876–1933) – a very strong and active personality – died, his body was mummified in the lotus position and committed to one of the chapels of the Potala. There he sat, wearing his ritual robes, in the room which one day would house his tomb. One day the monks watching over the body noticed that the head of the mummy was turning to the East. The lamas saw this as a clear indication of the direction in which they were to seek the new body. Moreover an old lama – a confidante of the dead man – saw in an intense dream a farmstead the roof of which was built in a remarkable way and which lay by a small, blue lake.

So a delegation of high lamas went eastwards with their escorts to look for this farmstead. And after about two years they found what they were looking for. By now they were in the region of Amdo, an area of Tibetan culture but one which had long been Chinese territory. That also explained the roof construction, which had green ceramic tiles in Chinese fashion.

Lamas and servants now exchanged clothes, and thus the delegation entered the farmstead. The supposed lamas were immediately offered the places of honour and the lamas dressed as servants waited in the courtyard with their mounts. Only a young boy who had been woken up was not deceived: he ran out into the courtyard and gave the lamas a warm welcome.

Now various objects were put in front of the boy, who was about two years old. There were new, colourful objects mixed with things from the possessions of the Thirteenth Dalai Lama. Without hesitating even for a moment, the child reached for 'his' things, and seemed to be particularly delighted about an old, well-worn prayer chain, which the Thirteenth Dalai Lama had been so fond of using.

The delegation was now convinced that it had found the 'new body', but difficulties arose. The Chinese had got wind of things and wanted to send a military 'guard of honour' made up of 3000 soldiers to Lhasa. This 'honour' could only be avoided by the payment of a large sum of money which first had to be got from Lhasa. Quite understandably, the messengers with the money could not travel along the usual – shortest – route since in all probability they would not have arrived. So it took some time to get the child and his family to Lhasa. There the body was subject to a further series of tests, the details of which have never been made known.

Now came a period of hard training for the small boy. Lamas were his teachers. He certainly did not have a childhood like others of his age. His parents and brothers and sisters could visit him sometimes, but such meetings were subject to strict ritual; after all the child was the Dalai Lama.

So this boy grew up in a period which was becoming

increasingly difficult. The Chinese invasion was on the horizon, and Maoist China did not disguise its intentions.

During the minority of the Dalai Lama a regent was responsible for affairs of state. He was clearly of an almost insuperable naivety. He simply would not see that the real danger was posed by the Chinese Popular Army of Liberation. In all seriousness it was believed that a tiny badly armed Tibetan army – if it could be called such – could defend Tibet successfully. Moreover the international isolation of Tibet, which over the centuries had regarded itself as a 'forbidden land', had its revenge. Thus the seriousness of the situation was recognized only at a late stage, and in 1950 an action began which for us is almost incomprehensible. There was a rush to enthrone the Dalai Lama, who was only fifteen. The Dalai Lama had to flee to India in 1951, but returned, hoping that the situation would improve. However, in 1959 he had finally to leave his country and again to flee to India.

From the beginning the Chinese occupiers saw themselves as the masters of Tibet. They forbade the growing of barley in Tibet on the grounds that wheat was substantially more nutritious. But they forgot that wheat can barely grow, if at all, at this height and with the prevailing climatic conditions. The result of this ordinance was a terrible famine which bears eloquent witness to a lack of sympathy and of all knowledge on the part of the Chinese rulers. (In the meanwhile the Chinese have proved more sensible; the Tibetans again cultivate barley for their tsampa and their beloved barley beer.)

The flight of the Dalai Lama in March 1959 was a dramatic affair: at this point in time he was in his summer residence of Norbulinka, in the 'garden of precious stones'. The situation was extremely tense; the Chinese had stationed massive forces in Lhasa. The army commandant now invited the Dalai Lama to a celebration at the Lhasa military base. He and his advisers inevitably saw the invitation in this situation as a trap, and the Dalai Lama refused it.

The tenseness of the situation was also clear to the people of the city and its surroundings. In a short space of time thousands of people formed a living ring around the summer palace to protect their kundun. But when the Popular Army of Liberation began to bombard Norbulingka, there was nothing left for the Dalai Lama but to flee. With those loyal to him, he succeeded in escaping from the summer palace by night and taking the road south towards India. A khampa particularly devoted to him – khampas are members of an East Tibetan tribe especially famous as warriors – formed the rearguard and certainly lost his life securing the river crossing. Now the Fourteenth Dalai Lama lives in exile in Dharamshala in northern India.

Since the Cultural Revolution, many thousands of Tibetans have had to flee their country; countless people have been carried off and many killed. This land on the roof of the world has paid a tremendous price in blood, and today large parts of the Tibetan population live scattered all over the world in a kind of diaspora. There are refugee camps all over India, in Switzerland, America, Italy, Spain, Germany, Austria and even Australia.

However, the faith of this people, its knowledge of the teaching of the Enlightened One who proclaimed his doctrine 2,500 years ago, is still unbroken. Still, some Tibetans have gone over to the opposite camp. Two prominent examples are the Panchen Lama (but see below) and a member of a Tibetan aristocratic family who is today a senior Communist official.

In honesty it should be noted here that after the end of the cultural revolution, religious practice in Tibet is freer than it used to be. Moreover the catastrophic devastations caused by the plundering revolutionary guards during the cultural revolution are gradually being repaired.

Believers can again be seen in the gompas, and as of old they are again going round the Barkhor, the 'sacred precinct' in Lhasa. However, the monks in the monasteries are officials of the 'Autonomous Region of Tibet in the People's Republic of China'. This is one way of controlling the number of monks in individual monasteries, since the number of 'officials' is regulated. However, in a conversation with me the Dalai Lama remarked that fewer and fewer monasteries are keeping to the number laid down by the authorities. Monks are still fleeing from Tibetan monasteries, since they have hardly any opportunity to get a really profound training there. But the Tibetans have refounded their monastic universities in India – near Bombay – and there the training which is still forbidden to them in Tibet is possible.

A few words about the Panchen Lama. The title was bestowed on the abbot of the Tasilhunpo monastery in Shigatse by the Fifth Dalai Lama in 1650. Panchen Lama is an abbreviation; the real title is Pandita Chen Pol, which is best translated 'great scholar'. As abbot of Tasilhunpo the Panshen Lama was also lord of the province of Tsang, which long had a special place in Tibetan politics. Clashes with the nobility of Lhasa often led to disputes.

After the occupation of Tibet by the Chinese, the Panchen Lama was under suspicion from his people, and even his authenticity was subject to doubt. It was said that in 1949, at the age of eleven he had written to Mao Tse Tung asking him to 'liberate' Tibet. However, after the 1959 uprising in Lhasa he protested to the Chinese about their atrocities and prophesied Tibet's future independence under the Dalai Lama. The result was that he was imprisoned for fourteen years, also suffering torture. He returned to Tibet in 1986 and died in 1989, finally regarded as a hero.

We have now moved from our real topic, Tibetan Buddhism, but the story of the Dalai Lama – and in particularly of the Fourteenth Dalai Lama, who is still alive today, is in the end part of Buddhist history. The Fourteenth Dalai Lama is a man who is open to the world; he has international stature and certainly plays a part in shaping the future destiny of a considerable part of present-day Buddhism.

In the Himalayan countries Buddhism encountered an animistic and shamanistic view of the world. This was not eradicated but largely incorporated into Buddhist views; demons and spirits became 'guardians of doctrine'. The Tibetan character, culture and tradition led to the formation of what is now called 'Tibetan Buddhism' or Lamaism. Tantric ideas have become mixed in with this world of Vajrayana, and they have sometimes even become normative. The special circumstances in Tibet led to the institution of the Dalai Lama. This 'theocracy' bound up with him was made possible and shaped by the reformation of the monasteries by Tsongkhapa and the foundation of the Gelugpa order.

8

Mantras and Mandalas and
the 'Book of the Dead'

Words and syllables are more than just a means of understanding; they say more and have further meaning.

'All that is visible is rooted in the invisible, the audible in the inaudible, the tangible in the intangible: perhaps also the conceivable in the inconceivable.' This saying by the great Western mystic Meister Eckhart shows us quite clearly that reflections which we engage in in connection with Buddhist thought also have roots in our own cultural circle: '. . . the audible in the inaudible' is the key to understanding the mantra. A word, a syllable, a single letter are not just exclusively superficial means by which people understand one another.

They are comparable with the melody of a song; a word can have meaning and expression over and above its plain form. This fact has often been forgotten, or banished to regions of the unconscious. But we still talk of the magical power of words. This magical power is not limited to the realm of poetry, but experience teaches us that it also plays a role in everyday life. It echoes in every word, every cry, every whisper.

Mantras are simply thoughts expressed aloud

There are many mantras, but here I shall investigate just one, the well known Om Mani Padme Hum, rather more closely. I shall deliberately not attempt to translate it, since this is certainly not the right way of bringing us nearer to its content. Here I am following – in abbreviated form and with slight modifications – an interpretation by Lama Anarika Govinda.

Om is 'the way to all things', the expression of the latent powers of the elements of earth and water, transformed into the higher form of plants. But these forces lie transformed in every creature and thus in every human being. Om is a way of expressing the human capacity for reflection; it is the sound equivalent for the external and internal form of speech. Om is the quintessence, the root syllable, in other words something like a grain of wheat which knows of its future form, its future being.

Mani stands for 'the way of becoming whole and identity of essence'. Mani is to be equated with the philosopher's stone and the blue flower of Western mystics and philosophical alchemists; it is the symbol of purity in its undifferentiated original form. Some writers identify mani with the 'jewel'. That only makes sense if by this we do not understand a precious stone that someone desires, but the 'diamond' (vajra) as the image of the indestructible, the absolute.

Padme is the 'way of developing vision'. The lotus blossom – from which the word derives – grows out of the darkness of the mud, breaks through the element of water, but once it blossoms remains untouched by both. So it is like the human spirit, which can raise itself from ignorance to the consciousness of enlightenment. The roots of humankind are in the dark depths of the world, but they can tower up into the bright fullness of knowledge.

Hum is the 'way of integrating fusion'. Om and Hum are complementary experiential values, perhaps comparable with the alpha and omega of Christian mysticism. In the Om we open ourselves up and in the Hum we surrender ourselves, for this is a sacrificial sound. Hum is the infinite in the finite, the eternal in the moment, the character in the circumstantial, the formless in the world of forms, the transcendent in the earthly, the wisdom of the 'great mirror', the sunyata, the void.

Here we have deliberately given ourselves over fully to mysticism, but this Om Mani Padme Hum, this mantra of the Avakoliteshvara, will now be something different for us from the usual translation 'The precious stone born in the lotus . . .'

Mention should be made of the Tibetan prayer wheels in this connection. These cylinders contain strips of paper – mostly prints from a monastery – with mantras or chapters from the Kangyur, the sacred scripture of Tibetan Buddhism. In the view of the faithful, the turning of this prayer cylinder – always clockwise – carries the mantra a thousandfold into the sphere of the Absolute. Western authors have dismissed this as 'mechanized piety' but we would do better to refrain from a verdict and thus a condemnation.

If one approaches a Tibetan monastery, one usually finds invisible 'signposts', the mani walls which are erected around the sanctuary. They consist of many thousands of mani stones, which have been piled up by pilgrims for generations. They have a mantra carved on them, usually the Avalokiteshavara's Om Mani Padme Hum. The believer will always go along a mani wall in such a way that his right shoulder is turned towards it. (During the Cultural Revolution the Chinese tore down these mani walls, above all in Lhasa, and used the stones for building roads!).

The nearer we come to a monastery, the more frequently we will find chörten – the Tibetan word for stupa – of different sizes. Today they are no longer shrines for relics, as was originally the case – above all under emperor Ashoka. The walled structures have a common ground plan. A cylindrical building, surmounted with an 'umbrella', is set on a square base with several steps leading up to it. Apart from this principle common to all of them, there is a series of differences in size, number of steps, proportion of the cylindrical part and colour. Each of these details has symbolic significance which the Tibetans can read off them. Some chörten can be entered and have colourful frescoes inside on which daylight never falls. Others are built as gates to holy precincts through which, for example, one enters the grounds of a monastery. There are also chörten which have four niches in their cylindrical part with Buddha figures pointing to the four points of the compass.

One special form of these buildings is the 'paper chörten'. This serves to contain scriptures which are no longer used, since Buddhists will never throw away anything written. So these scriptures which have been worn out and become unusable are kept in special chörten until one day they go mouldy and thus once again enter the cycle of nature.

Mandalas are aids to meditation and not real objects of worship

A mandala is an object usually in the form of a cross with a central figure and four 'doors' connected with the four points of the compass. Through various 'stations', by contemplating such a mandala the person meditating guides his mind to its centre, identifying with the symbolic figure on it. We find mandalas as paintings on the walls of gompas, on thangkas, and on prayer banners. As I have already indicated, many are basically nothing but three-dimensional mandalas.

There is yet another special kind of such an object, the

initiation mandala. Suppose we take a monastery somewhere in the Himalayas. If a getsul, a pupil monk, is to be
consecrated gelong, his lama, his teacher and spiritual
guide, gives him his own personal mandala for his future
life. He usually makes it on the ground with coloured grains
of barley and gives his pupil a last ceremonial lesson. The
young monk then meditates on this mandala and stamps it
indissolubly on himself. Then it is destroyed and from now
on lives on only in the mind of the newly ordained monk.

The yantra is a special form of mandala. This no longer
portrays figures, but makes use exclusively of geometrical
drawing. Circles, triangles, squares and right angles – and
sometimes also ellipses – provide a whole to direct the
person meditating.

The idea underlying the mandala and the yantra was
taken over from Hinduism and refined. But in the end this
notion is common to all cultures; the circle and the
structures pointing to the centre are age-old human
symbols. The rose window of a Gothic cathedral could be
taken as an example.

The dead return to the cycle of the elements

We keep hearing about the 'frightful', 'barbaric' funeral
customs of Tibetan Buddhism. Only abbots and other very
exalted persons are burned after their death; the usual form
of funeral is 'sky burial'. The dead person is taken to a
certain place, cut to pieces and left to the goats and wolves.

This may not seem very pious to us, but we should
remember that wood is scarce and is needed for the living.
Moreover there is no place for burials: cultivable land is too
rare and valuable, and all other land hardly allows burials, if
at all. Furthermore, people there see 'sky burials' as quite
normal. In this way the dead person returns to the cycle of
elements, the cosmos, the everlasting coming to be and

passing away in the world of the earthly. We too hear that we shall 'return to the dust of which we are made'.

The sites of 'sky burials' stir peoples' imaginations in the same way as our cemeteries do. Popular belief sees spirits and demons there, full of wild hatred and evil. Often these bloodthirsty demons take the form of Ildris, the snow leopard. However, this predatory beast, which has now become rare, really does exist up there on the plateaus of Tibet.

A ritual allegedly still practised today, the chod, demonstrates how Buddhist ideas can change and how much elements of the pre-Buddhist Bön can again come to the fore. A monk who has prepared for this event for years, spends many days and nights alone in such a place of 'sky burials', and there offers himself to the demons as a sacrifice. He asks them to make use of his body and blood; this is what seems a strange act of self-sacrifice. One can imagine what such a young man experiences in his ecstasy; he is in danger of losing his reason. And it may be that a hungry snow leopard will finish him off.

However, it would be quite wrong and misleading if one were to regard the conjuration of spirits and demons – or even the chod rite sketched out here – as characteristic of Buddhism. Here again it is animistic and shamanistic features which break through and overgrow the 'teaching of the Enlightened One'.

The 'Tibetan Book of the Dead'

The 'Tibetan Book of the Dead' probably also contains shamanistic and magical elements. This title, which is customary in the West, is hardly a happy one, since it does not get to the heart of the matter. In Tibet people call it the Bardo Thodol. Bardo means 'intermediate state'. That denotes the period which lies between the death of a person and his rebirth. The Tibetan word Thos Grol – pronounced Thodol – is best rendered 'liberation through understanding'. There are various such scriptures, some of them accessible to us in translation, though it should be remembered that transcriptions of such texts are always difficult and also carry risks of falsification. Knowledge of Vajrayana mysticism and Buddhist thought generally are probably indispensable for reading the Bardo Thodol.

The Bardo, the 'between', and the visions which appear in it, cannot be regarded either as popular superstition or as theoretical speculation. They are 'productions' of meditation, reflections of inner processes and states of mind attained by a lifelong training in meditation, which become visible. That means that people have to occupy themselves with the writings of the Bardo Thodol even during their lifetimes. So they are more a 'book of the living' than of the dead.

In the phase of dying the Lama calls up the pictures already formed by the dying person in his life. The visions of the 'peaceful' and 'terrifying' beings act like a protection against the terrors of dying and the threat of slipping away into lower spheres of existence. For these people rebirth is not a speculation, but simply a given fact.

So when the Lama begins each chapter of the Bardo Thodol with the words 'Hey, noble one!', he is conjuring up inner experiential values which were realized in life.

Hey! Now when the life between dawns upon me,
I will abandon laziness, as life has no more time,
Unwavering, enter the path of learning, thinking and meditating,
And taking perceptions and mind as path,
I will realize the Three Bodies of Enlighenment!
This once that I have obtained the human body
Is not the time to stay on the path of distractions.

In dying, first of all the 'primal light' appears. The one who is spiritually advanced will recognize it as such and in this moment he will attain illumination, become a Buddha and enter nirvana. But if someone is still caught in the dense net of his karma, he will be granted visions which come from himself, from his own karma, and are conditioned in this.

> 'Now the vision of all the five clans and the vision of the joining of the four wisdoms have come to escort you in their direction. Recognize them!'

Time and again in the course of the appearances and visions the possibility opens up of leaving the bhava chakra, the 'wheel of rebirth', through knowledge. The lama urgently points out to the departing person the opportunities offered to him, and time and again admonishes him to 'avoid the gloomy light'.

But then – so strong is the thirst and desire for being an life – the 'terrifying aspects' spring up from the consciousness of the one who is in Bardo, in the 'between'. The lama keeps assuring the dying person that he need have no anxiety: the terrifying figures come from himself; they are not real but products of our own karma.

The further the bardo progresses, the more urgently the lama warns against the greed that will lead this man to fall blindly into a new karma-conditioned existence. Now his yidams, his guardian spirits, appear to him. They too are not real, but come from his own depths.

A very important part of the Bardo Thodol is concerned with the 'transfer of consciousness'. This 'transfer of consciousness' is a Tantric practice which largely escapes our thought. It should be undertaken in youth, but at the latest when a person is in the process of striving for a wider being. It is a yoga technique which is connected with the Dhyani Buddha Amitabha and his 'radiant light'. Hig is the guiding mantra for this psychological-physical event. It has the aim of so preparing the uppermost exit at the top of the skull, the fontanelle, so that at death it is possible for the consciousness to depart unhindered.

Here we are moving in a sphere against which our thought and our experience react very strongly, though present-day depth psychology can recognize here archetypal processes of our sub-conscious.

The state of Bardo usually lasts forty-nine days. As the body cannot usually be kept as long as this, it is replaced by a picture or represented symbolically.

The Buddhist has no concept of a personal soul. What is incarnate in the next life is not a particular, defined personality but its karmatic impulse. The configurations of karma live on, but not an individuality. I have already mentioned the trulkus, who are an exception here.

The Bardo Thodol is a 'treasure text'. This term is applied to writings attributed to Buddha himself. Then, however, they remain hidden for centuries. Only when men have progressed enough spiritually to be able to understand them do they reappear, to give help on the way of salvation. There are many such' treasure texts', and the Buddhists of the 'thunderbolt vehicle' are convinced that yet others will emerge.

Mantras are 'non-syllables', spoken as it were 'between the tones and the sounds'. Mandalas and yantras are aids to meditation in two or three dimensions which lead the mind of the person meditating to the centre through spiritual stations. They are pointers by which the person meditating is to identify with the centre, the Absolute. The funeral customs of the Tibetans, the 'sky burials', take into account not only the philosophy of the unity of all being, but also the local conditions. The Bardo Thodol is not a 'Tibetan Book of the Dead', but rather a yoga technique which is usually practised all life long.

9

Buddhism and the West in the Twentieth Century

If it was the holy simplicity of faith which once heaped up pyres to burn 'heretics', now it is the holy simplicity of science (Christian Morgenstern).

In this book we have moved from considering the principles of Buddha Shakyamuni to the difficult Tantric ideas in Vajrayana Buddhism. The question may arise what all this can mean to us. To put it in the language of Westerners: What can we get out of it? What advantages can we gain from it?

If we look through the prospectuses of the various travel firms, we can see how incredibly easy it is to move physically into another world. Thus thousands of people from Europe and America make pilgrimages through the temples of Nepal, Thailand, China, Burma, Sri Lanka and India. The stupa of Borobodur in Java – a gigantic three-dimensional mandala – is like other such sites, more or less a museum, and our cameras catch 'exotic themes'. And there it remains.

Now a gigantic hotel has been opened in the 'Forbidden City', Lhasa, on the sacred precinct, and in the monasteries one can buy sacred objects and thangkas, some of them cheap forgeries. However, foreign tourism brings currency into the country. When I expressed my reservations, a Tibetan nobleman – today he is a Communist – said in good English: 'Why shouldn't we share in the profits from foreign trade? That's what you do. Is Tibet always to remain the poorhouse of the Republic of China? We want progress here.' Can one really contradict such a person?

The Dalai Lama made this comment on the sale of sacred objects and thangas – probably stolen: 'It is certainly regrettable if such things are taken, but it does have quite positive aspects. It may be that somewhere and sometime Europeans or Americans looking at a thankgka may feel that it says something to them.'

The present Dalai Lama is also absolutely positive about foreign tourism: 'People get to know one another, to understand one another.' Here one can certainly find optimism.

The question remains whether tourists who 'consume' a foreign culture with little or no preparation do not also bring negative influences into the country as well as money. Our ideas of happiness and a full life are what they are. Can they also be valid for the poor people, for example, on the Himalayan plateau? Have we anything to give, anything worth giving, other than in the material sphere?

But how is it the other way round? Has the Buddhist view of life of which I have only been able to give an incomplete sketch here anything to say to us? We people from Western civilization would probably be ill advised to become, for example, Vahrayana Buddhists. In addition to the indisputable fact that we simply could not, our commandment must be to cope with the life in which we are put. It cannot be our aim to escape from this 'civilized' life. Nevertheless, one could imagine that ideas from Buddhist philosophy could fit almost without a break into our time and our world.

The notion of karma as the universal personal responsibility of individuals towards themselves, their fellows and their environment is worth consideration, particularly by civilized people. Such a basic attitude could help to solve many problems. Moreover the basic notion does not go so much against traditions in which we have grown up as might appear at first sight. The impressive tolerance of Buddhist thought which often seems to us to be a lack of opinions is its strength. The lack of tolerance in our own society is undeniably its weakness. It should be generally acknowledged that tolerance is not unopinionated toleration, unthinking and uncritical endurance of the other. Rather, it is conscious strength derived from an extended consciousness, from an inner knowledge of the unity of all the phenomena of life. Only authentic inner certainty can beget tolerance, and never its opposite. Intolerance grows out of weakness.

Times are changing. Whereas until a few years ago Westerners unconditionally believed in their superiority and regarded the others as 'poor, uncivilized and un-cultivated barbarians', believing that they had to bring them the blessings of the West – if need be with force of arms or commerce – , we must note that in the meantime we have quite seriously begun to doubt this misguided attitude. Slowly but surely the recognition is being established in us that material possessions and human happiness do not necessarily go together, and that 'growth' and continual 'progress' are ultimately mirages. More and more people feel that things cannot go on like this. As a result of inexorable specialization we have been able to achieve great things in the sphere of technology. But human – and thus social – developments have got stuck. The holistic thought of Buddhism could in some respects be a pointer here. Our way cannot and should not lead back, but we are shaping the future here and now.

Our arrogant ideas of superiority led to the 'way inwards' being concealed for people. Not only was the term 'esoteric' forgotten, it also became disreputable and had – as it still has today – negative connotations. What can someone who lives in an interior way do in a society concerned with production and consumption? Such a person cannot be a useful member of this society which is so successful and so used to success.

Buddhist thought could help to heal our boundless concern with ourselves. It could and should give us the stimuli we so urgently need if one day we are not to slip into an inferno – perhaps even mass annihilation. The human being as the 'centre of all being' has become questionable, and we must learn again that we are part of a whole, that the harmony of this whole cannot be denied with impunity. Not Buddhism as a religious institution but the thoughts of Buddhist philosophy could offer us 'rich' civilized people help: tolerance, knowledge of our involvement in a whole and the responsibility for the totality bound up with this and our relation to nature in the broadest sense of the word as the matrix of any being.

In the first chapter I quoted the Fourteenth Dalai Lama on the problem of Western Buddhism. It is clear that Westerners must and should be able to incorporate new ideas into their own traditions, their own cultural sphere. They have neither reason nor occasion to break with this tradition or even to denigrate it. But in the quest for new ideas – I am deliberately avoiding the term ideologies – thoughts of the Buddha are still to be commended to some degree, since they are universal and undogmatic. And if we look at them more closely, they are not in conflict with the ethical maxims of the West. Nor do I share the view of various Western authors that Buddhism is a passive philosophy of extinction. This is quite clearly a misunderstanding of the striving of Buddhists for nirvana, though it must be conceded that this concept is in fact difficult for our Western understanding to grasp. It is probably best seen as a state of harmony in the universal sphere.

Finally let us listen once again to Buddha Shakyamuni: 'Imagine a man found an old path in the jungle. He followed it and discovered an old city which had formerly been inhabited by people. He reported this to the king, and he had it rebuilt so that it was populated again and flourished once more. In precisely this way I have found an old path: that trodden by the Buddhas of past time to nirvana' (Samyuta Nikaya).

It is quite possible that thoughts of Siddharta Gautama Buddha could also offer some help even to Westerners to cope with their problems. Mention should be made here above all of tolerance and the knowledge that human beings are involved in a totality. However – and again one should note the words of the Dalai Lama – we need to find a synthesis with our own traditions and our own culture. Little or nothing has been achieved if we seek to imitate rituals and cults which necessarily must be alien to us. It certainly cannot hurt us people of the West to be more preoccupied than before with other cultures, religions and ways of thought. This leads to a worthwhile extension of our consciousness without drugs and other harmful interventions. The mere widening of our horizon will help us on our way to the future. Buddhist ideas are just one of many possibilities.

Glossary

Avalokiteshvara	Tibetan 'Chenvesi', boddhisattva of compassion and mercy. The Dalai Lama is an incarnation of Avalokiteshvara.
Bardo	Form of existence between death and rebirth. Usually put at forty-nine days.
Bardo Thodol	Literally 'liberation through understanding in the Between'. The so-called Tibetan Book of the Dead, which derives from the Padmasambhava.
Bhakti	Leading concept in Mahayana, to be translated dedication (dedication to one's fellow human beings).
Bhava chakra	'Wheel of life', pictorial representation of the six spheres into which a person can be born.
Bhikku	Tibetan 'gelong'. Monk, member of the sangha (monastic community).
Bodhisattva	1. Being destined for illumination (Buddahood); 2. Enlightened One who voluntarily remains on the 'wheel of life' in order to help others on the way to Enlightenment.

Bön	Literally 'summon': collective term for various pre-Buddhist religions in the Himalayan countries.
Ch'an Buddhism	Chinese form of Mahayana hostile to dogmas and ritual; in Japan became Zen Buddhism.
Dalai Lama	Title of the Tibetan ruler bestowed by the Mongol Altan Khan in 1577; 'earthly birth' of Chenresi.
Dharma	1. Absolute law of the cosmos; 2. teaching of Buddha.
Dhyani Buddhas	Five 'meditating Buddhas' as aspects of the enlightened consciousness.
Eightfold Path	An essential element of the preaching of Buddha in Sarnath.
Four Noble Truths	Part of Buddha's preaching of principles in Sarnath.
Gautama	Name of the historical Buddha from the family of Shakya.
Getsul	Literally 'one who lives virtuously', disciple of a monk.
Gompa	Tibetan for Vihara, designation for a monastery.
Hinayana	'Little vehicle' in Buddhism today as Theravada Buddhism in South East Asia.
Karma	Literally 'action'. Causal principle which indwells beings, law of cause and effect.
Kundun	Literally 'presence', form of address to the Dalai Lama.
Lama	Teacher, spiritual master. Title of the Tibetan monastic hierarchy.

Lamaism	Designation of Tibetan Buddhism usual in the West.
Mahavira	Prophet of the Jain religion, a contemporary of Buddha.
Mahayana	The 'great vehicle' in Buddhism. In the form of Ch'an Buddhism in China and from there it went to Japan as Zen schools.
Mandala	Literally 'circle', 'bow': symbolic representation of cosmic forces; aid to meditation.
Mantra	Syllable loaded with power, a 'means which protects the spirit'. Mantras are regarded as sounds of cosmic energy.
Maya	Illusion of being with reference to the self as an independent truth.
Nirmanakaya	Body of the Buddha active on earth in the doctrine of three bodies (trikaya).
Nirvana	Also Mahapari-nirvana. State in a form of existence without polarity: Buddhahood.
Panchen Lama	A title bestowed on the abbot of the monastery of Shigatse from the Fifth Dalai Lama on.
Potala	Palace, temple and mausoleum complex in Lhasa, winter residence of the Dalai Lama.
Puja	Sacrificial action, prayer at sacrifice.
Red-hat order	Term used in the West for the non-reformed schools of Tibetan Buddhism (Nyingmapa, Kagyupa, Sakyapa, Kadampa).

Samsara	Cycle of birth; earthly life in the non-absolute sphere, governed by karma.
Sarnath	Present-day Isipatana near Benares (Varanasi) on the Ganges. Place where Buddha first preached his doctrine.
Shakya	Princely family from which Buddha came, hence Buddha Shakyamuni.
Shenrab	Reformer of the Bön, hence also called the Buddha of the Bön.
Siddharta	Name of the one who was later to become Buddha as son of Prince Suddhodana.
Songtsen Gampo	King of the Tibetan Yarlung dynasty (609–649); Buddhism began to get a foothold in Tibet under his rule.
Suddhodana	Prince and 'father' of Siddharta, later to be Buddha Shakyamuni.
Sunyata	The 'absolute void', the Absolute in itself, symbol of dharma.
Sutra	Writings of the Buddhist tradition.
Tantrism	Doctrinal system of extension of consciousness or attainment of illumination; way of redemption which makes use of the human capacity for experience.
Thangka	Illustrated scroll with religious content, help to meditation. Painted on material.
Trulku	Transformed body, 'magical body', incarnation of a saint.

Tsampa	Popular food in Tibet, barley flour with yak-butter tea.
Ü	Central province of Tibet, capital Lhasa.
Vajrayana	'Thunderbolt vehicle' in Buddhism; often synonymous with Tantrayana or Lamaism.
Wheel of Life	Symbol. Depiction of Buddha's preaching in Sarnath, usually a wheel with eight spokes, flanked by gazelles.
Yab-yum	Mother-father: symbolic representation of mystical sexual union, a symbol of the abolition of polarity.
Yellow-hat order	Gelugpa school in Tibetan Buddhism, founded by Tsongkhapa.
Yoga	Techniques for expanding consciousness derived from Hindu ideas through controlling bodily functions: body and spirit are to become a unity; the thinking self comes to a standstill or is detached from time and space and this leads to final redemption.

For further reading

E. Conze, *Buddhist Scriptures*, Penguin Books 1959

H. Dumoulin, *Buddhism in the Modern World*, Macmillan 1976

P. Harvey, *An Introduction to Buddhism*, Cambridge University Press 1980

Christmas Humphreys, *Buddhism*, Penguin Books ³1962

A. Kennedy, *The Buddhist Vision*, Rider 1985

Trevor Ling, *The Buddha*, Penguin Books 1973

Michael Pye, *The Buddha*, Duckworth 1979

R. H. Robinson and W. L. Johnson, *The Buddhist Religion*, Wadsworth ³1982

John Snelling, *The Elements of Buddhism*, Element Books 1990

The Tibetan Book of the Dead, translated by Robert A. F. Thurman, Aquarian/Thorson 1994

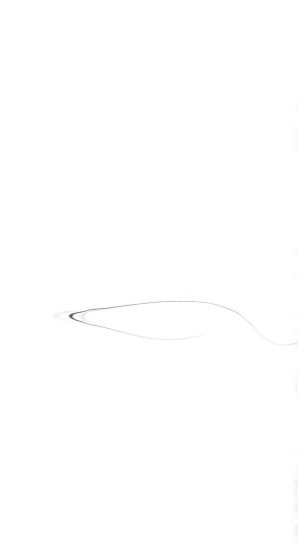